THE MEANING OF
ADULT EDUCATION

THE MEANING OF ADULT EDUCATION
EDUARD C. LINDEMAN

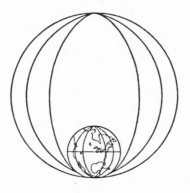

*Author of: The Community
and Social Discovery*

*Preface to the 1989 Edition
Huey B. Long*

*Preface to the 1961 Edition
J. R. Kidd*

OKLAHOMA RESEARCH CENTER FOR CONTINUING PROFESSIONAL AND HIGHER EDUCATION

For information address Oklahoma Research Center for Continuing
Professional and Higher Education
University of Oklahoma, Norman, Oklahoma 73037-0003.

Cover illustration by Allan Harrison.

Printed in the United States of America by Printing Services, The
University of Oklahoma, Norman, Oklahoma 73019-0445.

To
ALFRED DWIGHT SHEFFIELD

CONTENTS

PAGE

EDITOR'S PREFACE TO 1989 EDITION XIII

EDITOR'S PREFACE TO 1961 EDITION ... XXV

FOREWORD XXXIX

I FOR THOSE WHO NEED TO BE LEARNERS 1

II TO THOSE WHO HAVE FAITH IN
INTELLIGENCE 11

III WITH RESPECT TO THE USE OF POWER .. 21

IV IN VIEW OF THE NEED FOR SELF-EXPRESSION 31

V FOR THOSE WHO REQUIRE FREEDOM 41

VI FOR THOSE WHO WOULD CREATE 51

VII TO THOSE WHO APPRECIATE 61

VIII TO AN AGE OF SPECIALISM 73

IX AS DYNAMIC FOR COLLECTIVE ENTERPRISE 91

X IN TERMS OF METHOD 107

POSTSCRIPT 125

REFERENCES 131

INDEX 137

EDITOR'S PREFACE TO 1989 EDITION

EDITOR'S PREFACE TO 1989 EDITION

The Meaning of Adult Education, written by Eduard Lindeman in 1926, is one of the more enduring publications released during the formative years of adult education in the United States. Both the book and the man have stimulated conversations of adult educators for more than sixty years. Numerous treatments of Lindeman's career exists. Brookfield (1987) identifies fourteen publications that focused on Lindeman between 1956 and 1987 excluding his 1987 book. In addition Rielly (1984) reports that Lindeman published an estimated 204 articles, 107 book reviews, 5 books, 16 monographs and 17 chapters in other works. In addition he edited 4 books, and shared joint authorship of another.

Despite the extent of scholarship by and about Lindeman, his ideas and comments upon adult education are often presented with little to no contextual discussion, e.g. they do not place Lindeman in his historical period or relate his ideas to popular ideas of the day. A recent exception is Fisher's (1989) report "Eduard Lindeman, the Social Gospel and Adult Education." In contrast, at least seven of the published items identified by Brookfield (1987) purport to link Lindeman's work with contemporary adult education philosophy and action. Unfortunately, because of the one-sided nature of speculation about Lindeman's scholarship Lindeman and *The*

Meaning of Adult Education take on an ahistorical character. In other words the origins of Lindeman's thoughts are usually ignored. The period in which he reached his chronological and intellectual maturity is seldom discussed. Such oversight is the more surprising considering Lindeman's own emphasis on the social context. For example, Brookfield (1987) failed to provide any observations about Lindeman's own social period even though he made the following comment about the importance of social forces to Lindeman. He said,

> . . . there was no such thing as a 'privatized' life style, nor could there be a me generation. Social living in the twentieth century was such that individuals were constantly brought into confrontation with institutions and political or economic forces which shaped their individual lives. . . . Like it or not, Lindeman argued, we are social creatures, and in the creation and operation of our social forms we can see the highest realization of our humanity. (Brookfield, 1987, n.p.)

Separation of Lindeman from his social context leads to erroneous attribution. Brookfield (1987), for example, in commenting upon Lindeman's use of 'the sociological imagination' attributes the 'invention' of the phrase to C. W. Mills. Actually, Mills did not invent the term as suggested by Brookfield. Bogardus (1960) indicates that Charles A. Ellwood used the term as early as 1923. Is it possible that Lindeman's ideas as expressed in *The Meaning of Adult Education* and other works were influenced by Ellwood and others?

Space will not permit an exhaustive dissertation upon Lindeman and his times here. However, lest we continue to contribute to the ahistorical image of Lindeman and compound erroneous views of him and his times, this Preface to the 1989 edition provides a brief biography of Lindeman and a description of the historical period preceding the publication of *The Meaning of Adult Education*. For a more complete biography please see David Stewart's (1987) *Adult Learning in America: Eduard Lindeman and His Agenda for Lifelong Education*.

Biography

Eduard Christian Lindeman was one of ten children. He was born in St. Clair, Michigan, on the ninth of May, 1885, to German immigrants, (not Danish as indicated by Kidd in the Preface to the 1961 edition). His parents, Frederick and Frederecka Johanna Von Piper Lindemann, died while Eduard was a youngster. Despite a difficult childhood that included little formal schooling and manual labor he somehow obtained admission to Michigan Agricultural College (later Michigan State University) in a special program for "sub-freshmen."

Lindeman appears to have undergone some psychologically stressful experiences that contributed to an identity problem. He changed his birth name, *Edward* Lindemann, and inconsistently spelled his name before eventually settling on Eduard Christian Lindeman (Stewart, 1987). While in college he combined a series of jobs on the college farm with his studies, which must have been challenging to someone who may have been nearly illiterate (Brookfield, 1987). Despite his disadvantaged background it appears that Lindeman could be very charming and possibly received tutorial assistance from several sources including a college secretary (Brookfield, 1987). The fact that the father of his college sweetheart, Hazel Taft, was the chairman of the college horticultural department probably did not interfere with his development.

Stewart indicates that the five years spent in college were busy ones for Lindeman. He was involved in numerous extra-curricular activities including the YMCA, a writing society he helped to form called the Penman, and another society he helped to found, the Ethnic-Sociological Society. Collectively these three organizations appear to represent important elements of Lindeman's thought and character.

Graduating at age 26 (1911) he took a job as editor of a Michigan agricultural journal *The Gleaner*. After only a year Lindeman returned to East Lansing to marry Hazel (1912) and remained in the East Lansing area until 1920. During those nine years he held a variety of jobs including serving as assistant minister of the Plymouth Congregational Church and extension director of Boys and Girls Clubs, later the 4-H Club. After a very successful tenure with the extension service some of his ideas, which may have been too liberal, conflicted with those of the organization and he lost his job. In 1920 he began his career as a college professor. His first professorship was a short and questionable tenure at the YMCA George Williams College in Chicago where once again his liberal views of social change created a problem. He then left Chicago for the North Carolina College for Women in Greensboro, N.C. Failing to find satisfaction in North Carolina he soon departed for the New York School for Social Work (Stewart, 1987).

Thus, in 1924, at the age of 39 Lindeman became professor of social philosophy at the New York School of Social Work. *The Meaning of Adult Education* published in 1926, was his fourth book (Brookfield, 1987): *College Characters: Essays and Verse* (1912), *The Community: An Introduction to the Study of Community Leadership and Organization* (1921), *Social Discovery: An Approach to the Study of Functional Groups* (1924). Between 1926 and his death in 1953 Lindeman published a variety of short and frequently loosely organized articles and edited a few books as noted previously. Only a small proportion of his publications deal with adult education. Of 165 of Lindeman's published works cited by Stewart (1987) 40 appear to focus directly on education of adults. Some of these relate to parent education, worker education, and group discussion. Many of the others deal with social work, social philosophy, social ethics, religious topics, and political subjects. It should not be forgotten that Lindeman was primarily a social worker turned philosopher and that his view of adult education was influenced accordingly. Some speculations concerning possible sources that influenced Eduard Lindeman's ideas about education of adults are noted in the following section.

Intellectual Heritage

Stewart (1987) indicates that John Dewey, William James and Charles Sanders Peirce probably inspired much of Lindeman's philosophy. However, possibly other intellectuals and significant contemporary events also enriched his ideas. Lindeman's birth preceded the Chicago Haymarket riots by no more than one year. He reached his maturity when social work and sociological explanations for group and individual behavior were enthusiastically accepted by liberals, progressives and intellectuals. Limited references to Lindeman's undergraduate years indicate that he may have developed an interest in the science of society. Recall he was a founding member of the Ethnic-Sociological Society. Stewart credits Lindeman, as editor of the college newspaper, with the responsibility for publishing an article by Professor W. O. Hedrick "in which he presented the fundamental facts about these studies (social science) of 'man's problems'" (Stewart, 1987, p. 21). By the time Lindeman graduated from college Progressivism was at a fever pitch. Education, science and efficiency were joined with organic views of society as popularized by Dewey, Holmes, Robinson and Veblen, a science of society, as promulgated by Lester Ward and social action based on earlier activities of settlement workers like Jane Addams. Fisher (1989) quotes Lindeman (1943) as commenting on the influence of Walter Rauschenbusch, a theologian, who is closely identified with the social gospel as follows: "I was one of his devoted admirers and without his knowledge he exercised a profound influence upon my life at a crucial moment." (p. 139).

If an individual's life, as theorized by Lindeman, is shaped by institutions, political ideas and economic forces, we cannot understand Lindeman and his thoughts about the meaning of adult education without an awareness of those forces during his lifetime. Therefore, the following summary of the period between 1885 and 1926 may help us to have a better appreciation for his thoughts.

Historical Context

Eduard Lindeman's first forty years were lived in one of the most tumultuous periods of recent American history. Major changes in business, ideology, immigration and labor mark the period. The social gospel and social work competed with Spencer's Social Darwinism. New immigrants from eastern Europe who settled in the nation's urban centers competed with older immigrants from western Europe. Agricultural populism in the

South and West added to the mixture. Labor fought bloody battles with management and militia. Such was the last decade of the nineteenth century that Commager (1970, p. 42) calls it: . . . the watershed of American history.

Education was perceived to be a key element by reformers who ranged across the ideological spectrum from the social gospel, to labor, to settlement workers, to the progressive middle-class. Some intellectuals, such as Washington Gladden and Josiah Strong, thought public education was a holding operation that would serve until other great forces could transform society. Franklin Giddings and Lester Ward, however, believed the schools had a central role in social change. They also believed that the schools were for adults as well as children. Nor did education, which would facilitate "the arrival of Social Rationality, preparing the nation for a higher civilization" (Wiebe, 1957, p. 157) end in the classroom. The social scientist Simon N. Patten "exhorted social workers to educate the poor. Social worker Peter Roberts urged trade unions to educate the immigrants, and Ward expected the State to educate everybody" (Wiebe, 1967, p. 157). Stewart (1987) indicates Patten may have been the first American to use the term "adult education" to refer to educational programs for mature adults.

It was in such an historical environment that Eduard Lindeman developed his philosophy of education and life. Even though details are missing, it appears that his experience in the church, the YMCA and youth work directly afforded him an opportunity to apply his philosophy in practical settings. Thus, he had a way of not only appreciating the thoughts of Addams, Dewey, Patten and Rauschenbusch, he also had the opportunity to see them applied.

The Meaning of Adult Education

Given the above description of Eduard Lindeman and his times we can perhaps have a deeper appreciation for *The Meaning of Adult Education*. We have a perspective of a young man whose childhood was marked by poverty and hard work. One who somehow was encouraged to take a tremendous risk in confronting an educational institution with which he had little or no familiarity. One who, despite great odds, was inspired to high levels of social and scholarly activity.

The Meaning of Adult Education provides contemporary students of adult education with a useful commentary on the topic. The fact that it is the perspective of an individual whose calling was in another area does not detract from its value. As adult educators persist in their struggle with definitions of adult education and of themselves, Lindeman's comments should continue to contribute to the conversation.

Therefore, we are pleased to have the opportunity for

the Oklahoma Research Center for Continuing Professional and Higher Education to publish the 1989 reprint edition as the second book in our program of reviving and reprinting selected classics in the field.

HUEY B. LONG
NORMAN, OKLAHOMA
MAY 9, 1989

REFERENCES

Bogardus, Emory S. (1960). *The Development of Social Thought* (Fourth Edition). New York: Longmans, Green and Co., Inc.

Brookfield, Stephen (1987). *Learning Democracy: Eduard Lindeman on Adult Education and Social Change.* Wolfeboro, New Hampshire: Croom Helm.

Fisher, James C. (1989). "Eduard Lindeman, the Social Gospel and Adult Education." *Proceedings of the Thirtieth Annual Adult Education Research Conference*, Madison, Wisconsin: University of Wisconsin–Madison, 139–144.

Lindeman, Eduard C. (1912). *College of Characters: Essays and Verse.* Port Huron, Michigan: Riverside Printing Co.

Lindeman, Eduard C. (1921). *The Community: An Introduction to the Study of Community Leadership and Organization.* New York: Association Press.

Lindeman, Eduard C. (1924). *Social Discovery: An Approach to the Study of Functional Groups.* New York: Republic Publishing Co.

Lindeman, Eduard C. (1943). *Faith for a New World.* Rochester, N.Y.: Colgate Rochester Divinity School.

Rielly, Edward (1984). "Eduard C. Lindeman: Self-Directed Learner for the Eighties." Proceedings of the Twenty-fifth Annual Adult Education Research Conference. Raleigh, N.C.

Stewart, David (1987). *Adult Learning in America: Eduard Lindeman and His Agenda for Lifelong Education.* Melborne, Florida: Kreiger Publishing Co.

EDITOR'S PREFACE TO 1961 EDITION

EDITOR'S PREFACE TO 1961 EDITION

With the passing of some men we are numbed. Which of us then alive can recall the moment we first heard of the death of President Roosevelt and not be reminded how we halted where we stood. We sensed we had reached the end of an era, and, for a moment at least, all of us, antagonist or partisan, were piercingly aware that our lives would never be the same again.

It is not so with all men, not even with all great men. When Eduard Christian Lindeman died we felt no such shock because, somehow, much of him lived and moved on. Those nearest him, who knew him best and longest, were deeply grieved. We all mourned him; we all missed him; but in a curious way there was little sense of irrevocable loss. Why was this?

Lindeman had finished some of the many things he had set out to do. To be sure, not all the courses that had attracted his bold spirit were run, there was still injustice to be fought, and the inhumane to be brought to bay — but he had completed much; affirmed much.

But others can justly claim a lifetime of accomplishment. A record of attainment does not explain the continuing "presence" that we feel about Lindeman. But there is little mystery about it. Lindeman's influence has been so widespread, his ideas have become so much the best part of us that, in a very real sense, there has been no ending, no parting. It's a remarkable form of immortality and one that would have moved him.

Lindeman's influence is all round; it is in the words spoken, and the attitude expressed at any national convention of social workers, or of civil liberties, or adult education, or workers education. Much of the "capital of ideas" that is operative in these fields, is, of course, *universal* but it became common currency through the voice and writing of Lindeman. And it is more than words or ideas, it is the spirit, the zest for learning. His was no gospel of compulsion, of rigidity, of self-mortification.

> Another educational fallacy... is the persistent belief that whatever else education may be it is at bottom a grim and burdensome business.... This belief in the antagonism between learning and pleasure is, of course, sheer nonsense. The contrary is nearer the truth; the delights of the mind are superior in quality to any other form of enjoyment. Intellectual acquisitions are, indeed, the only forms of wealth which once attained and used can never be lost — which do not lose their luster with time.[1]

But while much of the best thought in adult education stems, in part at least, from Lindeman, he is a *contemporary*, not a historical figure. We now present *The Meaning of Adult Education* not as an eloquent statement of genuine historical value (which it is) but for its power to illuminate the present and reveal the future.

1. Gessner, Robert, Editor, *The Democratic Man, Selections from the writings of Eduard C. Lindeman,* Boston, Beacon Press, 1956, p. 152.

EDITOR'S PREFACE TO 1961 EDITION

When the adult education associations of the United
Kingdom, the United States and Canada combined in
1956 to bring about a reprinting of the famous *1919
Report* under the title *Design for Democracy* the most
perceptive critics observed that it must have been written
"just for this moment". So it is with Lindeman.

Like Walt Whitman, whatever Lindeman did or said
was somehow an expression of, and a search for, the
democratic vision. This has been well expressed in a
splendid collection of Lindeman's writings edited by his
son-in-law, Robert Gessner, and published by the Beacon
Press under the appropriate title *The Democratic Man*.
At a time when as a Federal Government administrator,
he had suffered all the perplexities and vicissitudes of
attempting to put his social ideas into practice, he wrote:

> Democracy turns out to be a conception of sove-
> reignty founded upon the assumption that ultimate
> power can only be safely trusted in the hands of the
> people, a conception of human equality based upon
> the assumption that basic human needs are similar
> and that these needs will be more readily satisfied
> through democratic rule than by any other method
> of governing, a conception of human relationships
> which move ideally from exploitive and mechanistic
> patterns towards mutual and organic patterns, and
> finally a conception of the inter-relatedness of all
> varieties of human experience.[2]

Note, this was not just the voice of a professor of
philosophy, it was wrung from a man who had had a

2. *Ibid.* pp. 53 and 54.

part in the frustrations and annoyances, the agonizingly slow progress of governing.

> Those who share this interpretation of democracy must, of course, admit at the outset that it represents an ideal which will never be realized in completion. Imperfect individuals cannot build perfect societies. The ideal character of the democratic idea should not, therefore, be used to its discredit. Health is also an ideal concept, and likewise beauty, intelligence, and efficiency. None of these ideals gets itself fully realized but this is not an argument on behalf of their abandonment....[3]

As well as, perhaps better than, anyone else, Lindeman understood the inter-relationship that must exist between study and action. The key word for him was always *participation*. Education must always form part of the equation of progress.

> Social action is in essence the use of force or coercion. The use of force and coercion is justified only when the force is democratic and this means that it must be derived from intelligence and reason. Adult education... turns out to be the most reliable instrument for social actionists. If they learn how to educate the adherents of their movement, they can continue to utilize the compelling power of a group and still remain within the scope of democratic behaviour. When they substitute something other than intelligence and reason, social action emanates as sheer power and soon degenerates into habits which tend toward an anti-democratic direction. Every social action group should at the same time be an adult education group, and I go even so far as to believe that all successful adult-education groups sooner or later become social-action groups.[4]

3. *Ibid.* p. 54.
4. *Journal of Educational Sociology*, September, 1945.

During the years when Thorndike, Lorge and others were assessing the physiological and psychological bases for *excellent* adult learning, Lindeman was describing the special character and the depth of mature learning. He did not look upon learning merely as some kind of social *governor* or control: primarily it was itself dynamic; essentially it meant change and growth. "You don't change," he once said, "until you do something. You don't change by listening. You don't change by talking. You actually change when something happens to your muscles. When you step or move in a new way, then the change becomes really significant."

These were the ideas being injected "into the mind and the bloodstream" both of adult education and social work during many critical formative years. Those, who could, travelled to New York to enroll in his classroom at the New York School of Social Work; those, who could not, became part of that larger classroom when, for three months or so every year, he would journey about North America and abroad, questioning, lecturing, teaching.

It was an unconventional classroom. He was an incisive questioner, and he encouraged, he demanded systematic and rigorous thinking. But in what other course in social philosophy might a student be given an assignment of going to Ebbetts Field (then the home of the famous Brooklyn Dodgers baseball team) and be told to

report on the behaviour and social values of that pheno-
menon. Or be read aloud to from Mark Twain, Aristotle,
1066 and all That and the Upanishads during the same
lecture. Or be afforded in class an eye-witness account
of the Sacco — Vanzetti trials by one of the defending
lawyers in order to reflect upon and argue about social
justice.

But Lindeman's own education had been unconventional. That is putting it mildly. His career is an exempli-
fication of the great and *true* democratic myth of the
power of education to transform a life. Once more we
are aware of the terrifying costs, paid both by the individual and by society, because of under-education. Throughout the world hundreds of millions of men and women
are illiterate; here in North America are millions who
are under-educated, incapable of coping well with life's
complexities and opportunities.

It is rather fascinating to think that two men who
epitomize the force and dynamism of education are Nikita
Kruschev and Eduard Lindeman. Both attended primary
school occasionally and spasmodically; both at age 21
were almost equally innocent of what formal schooling
ought to give to any youth; both have made extraordi-
nary use of their opportunities for education in adult
life.

If ever our concern for extending education to any
and every adult ever cools; if ever we tend to accept the

ignorant judgement of those who cry "What's the use?" or "It's too late!" we ought to remind ourselves of the muscular, shambling, shrewd but ignorant youth, encumbered by a past of misfortune and failure, and doomed to further failure that arrived at Michigan State University.

When the chance did come to Lindeman, after the first awkward stage when he must have been a trial to himself and to his teachers, his passion, his appetite for books and learning was gargantuan. Years later he wrote:

> My interest in reading is perhaps accentuated by the fact that the written word entered my life at so late an age. My formal education began at the age of twenty-one. I proceeded to immerse myself in the sea of books and after forty-five years of hungry reading, I still find no greater delight. I wonder if you can imagine the sensation of entering the world of literature having already reached maturity! I still feel a haunting sense of wonder in the presence of a book. How did it come into being? What agonies must not the author have suffered before allowing his words to become public property.[5]

No triumph in his later years pleased him more than the success of the *Mentor* books, a series which he conceived and for which he served as advisory editor. His family well remember this period: "The mornings he dressed to attend editorial sessions were happy mornings;

---

5. "The Contribution of Low Cost Books to American Culture", an address by Lindeman to Stephens College, Missouri, January 18, 1951.

he was sailing forth to select books which would be read by millions."

But could anyone be less what is termed bookish, than Lindeman. Books to him were an expression of life but he was never obliged himself to live vicariously. During his life-time he had many jobs and avocations — ship-builder, farm hand, varsity fullback, nurseryman, poet, journalist, assistant to a clergyman, youth counsellor, teacher and professor, group leader, federal government official.

Books were invaluable instruments to him but his approaches to the solution of problems were many and varied. For a year or so I served him as a kind of class librarian; the duties were slight and the opportunity to put questions to him that perplexed me was irresisti-ble. Once in the early years of my work with the Canadian Association for Adult Education I went to New York to consult him about a difficult new enterprise on which we were embarking. I half-expected him to recommend a dozen books and references. Instead he said I must accompany him to Forest Hills to watch some cham-pionship tennis matches. During the four hours in the sunshine we talked little of my problem, but when the long afternoon was over, somehow it no longer seemed so difficult to solve.

While he might be termed an *idealist,* Lindeman had a tough practical core. He knew that progress did not come by thinking, wishing or by chance. Work was needed and conflict was certain. He never hated men but he had a deep and abiding loathing for injustice. Teaching social philosophy was never enough for him; he must himself take part where the battle was fiercest and where brave spirits quailed. Lindeman was a frequent target for abuse and calumny; he was driven from one post for treating men of colour simply as men. He defined a social philosopher as a person "who genuinely cares for human beings and their welfare, who strives to include factual material taken from the social sciences as basic components of his thought and who is seeking appropriate avenues of social change.... It is practically impossible to play the role of social philosopher without assuming the hazard of social action. It is of the essence of social philosophy that facts, values and actions shall somehow be blended." A front-line fighter in many civil liberties campaigns, he often knew the bitterness of defeat.

> Wisdom is not the only ingredient which determines social issues. Greed, ignorance, stupidity and downright ill will are also involved, and among these negatives, the philosopher's virtues must shine. The hazards are real and formidable.... And there will be disappointments, tragic even to the limits of utter failure.[6]

He ended by teaching philosophy but his earlier teaching had been in sociology. Lindeman was several decades

---

6. From the "Foreword", by Max Otto, in *The Democratic Man,* p. 5.

ahead of his time in understanding the importance of small groups; his early books *The Community: an introduction to the study of community leadership and organization* (1921) and particularly *Social Discovery: an approach to the study of functional groups* (1924) are indispensable classics of the same order as the books of Mary Follett with whom, at a later stage, he collaborated. Occupied as he always was with the application of science and reason, his deepest concern was with the development and expression of goodness, which he always attempted to define in practice. In his very last year he spoke of the good man as one who

- does not posit perfectionism as a goal.
- does not try to live by extremes, avoids false antitheses.
- does not resort to blame-fixing, persecution, hatred.
- does not anticipate release from conflict but strives to elevate the conflict in which he is involved to higher levels.
- knows how to live and work in and through groups, but steadfastly refuses to become collectivized, "groupized", that is completely, subservient to the group.
- never abandons the right to dissent.
- is capable of utilizing humour as a perspective.
- does not permit himself to be used as means to external ends, nor resorts to the use of others as means.
- feels no compulsion to assume superiority over others and consequently no compulsion to treat others as inferiors.
- persists in believing and acting as though the human enterprise were an everlasting experiment in which the outcome is uncertain and contingent but a continuing adventure, an exciting exploration.[7]

---

7. "Education and the Good Life", an address by Lindeman to the Kilpatrick Conference, November 17, 1951.

In speech and writing he was often so direct and lucid that some disparaged him as simple, just as Socrates was disparaged.

In any single year Lindeman might appear in twenty or thirty different states. He was often in Canada, occasionally in Europe, and spent some memorable months in India. His visits to Denmark, the homeland of his parents, first in 1920, affected him profoundly as is clear from the present book.

We have selected *The Meaning of Adult Education* as the first in a series of books that will be addressed to that company of adult educationists that are now found in every part of the world and whose common purposes were expressed in the *Montreal Declaration,* endorsed without a single dissenting vote, at the UNESCO World Conference on Adult Education in 1960, which says in part:

> The destruction of mankind and the conquest of space have both become technological possibilities in our present generation.... Our first problem is to survive. It is not a question of the survival of the fittest; either we survive together, or we perish together. Survival requires that the countries of the world must learn to live together in peace. "Learn" is the operative word. Mutual respect, understanding, sympathy are qualities that are destroyed by ignorance and fostered by knowledge. In the field of international understanding adult education in today's divided world takes on a new importance.[8]

---

8. Report of The World Conference on Adult Education, Paris, Unesco, 1961.

We believe that *The Meaning of Adult Education,* published in 1926, and out of print for more than three decades, breathes the same spirit and illuminates the same theses as does the Montreal Declaration. We are grateful to Hazel Taft Lindeman for permission to bring her husband's book before a larger audience.

Wherever we have travelled we have heard favorable references to *The Meaning of Adult Education,* usually by those who have never seen it in full. But it is a sorry fate for a fine book to be "referred to with respect". It ought to be read.

J. R. KIDD,
Toronto, 1961.

FOREWORD

FOREWORD

"EACH OF US," wrote Anatole France, "must even be allowed to possess two or three philosophies at the same time," for the purpose, I presume, of saving our thought from the deadly formality of consistency. No one can write about education, particularly adult education, without deserting at various points all "schools" of pedagogy, psychology and philosophy. Incongruities are obvious: one cannot, for example, be a determinist and at the same time advocate education; nor can idealism be made to fit the actualities of life without recognition of the material limitations which surround living organisms. One cannot, that is, make use of these opposed points of view if they are conceived to be mutually-exclusive. But it is precisely because I do not so regard them that all are included in this essay. Light comes from learning—just as creation comes everywhere—through integrations, syntheses, not through exclusions.

The essay which follows will be best understood in the light of personal experience. My formal education began at the age of twenty-one—after I had spent twelve years in various occupations and industries. I could, of course, speak the English language (at least, the Americanized version which workers used) but it was not my natural medium of communication. My initiation to formal education was, next to the unsuccessful attempt to adjust myself to automatic machines, the most perplexing and baffling experience of my existence. The desire somehow to free education from stifling ritual, formalism and institutionalism was probably born in those frantic hours spent over books which mystified and confused my mind. I had already earned my way in the world from the age of nine, had learned the shipbuilding trade, had participated in strikes, and somehow none of the learning I was asked to do seemed to bear even the remotest relation to my experience. Out of this confusion worse confounded (confounded confusion, some one has called it) grew the hope that some day education might be brought out of college halls and into the lives of the people who do the work of the world. Later I came to see that these very people who perform productive tasks were themselves creating the experience out of which education might emerge.

In 1920 I visited Denmark, not primarily to study education but to pick up lost ancestral threads—a quest which arose from my dislocated youth. Here I came into contact with a civilization which, by sheer contrast with hate-ridden Europe, seemed like a cultural oasis in the desert of nationalism. Whereas the victorious nations were grasping for territory, Danish statesmen were conducting a scientific study to determine how much of Schleswig-Holstein might be regarded as being integral to Denmark. All of it was within their reach, for Germany

[xl]

was incapable of making effective protest even through the doubtful means of plebiscites; they, the Danes, wanted not what overheated nationalism might have demanded but merely what scientific research could validate. And then I saw farmers studying in people's colleges (Volkshochschulen), studying for the purposes of making life more interesting; these same farmers were members of comprehensive coöperative enterprises—dairies, creameries, cheese-factories, egg-shipping associations, slaughtering-plants, banks, stores, insurance societies, et cetera— enterprises which performed so many economic functions that the farmers were freed for other activities; and there could be found neither wealth nor poverty in the land.[1] Here, it seemed to me, was a culture which included many of the attributes which have been desired since the time of the early Greeks; besides, it was founded upon rigorous science and a degree of economic freedom —both of which were absent in Greek culture.

Beneath the easily-recognizable distinctions in Danish life—collective economic organization, interest in literature, art and recreation, absence of imperialism, et cetera— one finds an educational ferment such as motivates no other people in the modern world. Since the days of Grundtvig, which were also the days of Denmark's material and spiritual impotence, Danish adults have striven to close "the yawning abyss between life and enlightenment." "What the enemy has taken from us by force from without, we must regain by education from within," they said and forthwith laid the foundations for a system of education which continues so long as life lasts. Adult education, one begins to learn after prolonged observation, has not merely changed citizens from illiteracy to literacy; it has rebuilt the total structure of life's values.

Can adult education do as much for us? Our situation is, obviously, out of range of comparison: we are a large nation in area and in population; we possess no homogeneous culture; and we have already become wealthy. In addition, we have become habituated to a method of achievement which is in essence antithetical to intelligence. We measure results quantitatively. We could have an adult education movement in America almost overnight; advertising psychologists and super-salesmen could "put it over" for us for a cash consideration. But, what gets "put over" never stays "put". The chief danger which confronts adult education lies in the possibility that we may "Americanize" it before we understand its meaning.

I have therefore chosen the theme: *The Meaning of Adult Education.* The topc is, obviously, preliminary. We shall discover *our* meanings when we are engaged in the process of adult education, not in advance. My treatment of the theme is also partial since I have, following the advice of Walt Whitman, "let myself go free." The material which composes this essay has been brewing for years but it has been formulated within a short space of time— short, that is, for one who is accustomed to aim at accuracy of statement. It goes forth, not primarily to explain and convince, but to challenge. I trust that proper credit has been given to those whose thought has stimulated mine.

"Greystone"
High bridge,
New Jersey.
August 1926.

I

FOR THOSE WHO NEED TO BE LEARNERS

"We need, then, to reintegrate, to synthesize, to bind up together the different forces and influences in our national life. We need a greater courage: seriousness, a greater courage in self-knowledge, a greater unity; and changes in the machinery of our education which leave our religious and political life in their existing incoherence, or even add to it, will not serve our purpose."

—A. E. ZIMMERN.

"The principle we wish to establish is that the important thing in this connection is an increased demand on the part of all kinds of people for educational facilities, which may roughly be termed non-vocational, since they are concerned really with restoring balance to a man who has, of necessity, developed to a great extent one or other of his characteristics for the purposes of his livelihood or for the satisfaction of his reasonable desires."

—ALBERT MANSBRIDGE.

FOR THOSE WHO NEED TO BE
LEARNERS

EDUCATION conceived as preparation for life locks the learning process within a vicious circle. Youth educated in terms of adult ideas and taught to think of learning as a process which ends when real life begins will make no better use of intelligence than the elders who prescribe the system. Brief and rebellious moments occur when youth sees this fallacy clearly, but alas, the pressure of adult civilization is too great; in the end young people fit into the pattern, succumb to the tradition of their elders—indeed, become elderly-minded before their time. Education within the vicious circle becomes not a joyous enterprise but rather something to be endured because it leads to a satisfying end. But there can be no genuine joy in the end if means are irritating, painful. Generally therefore those who have "completed" a standardized regimen of education promptly turn their faces in the opposite direction. Humor, but more of pathos lurks in the caricature of the college graduate standing in cap and gown, diploma in hand, shouting: "Educated, b'gosh!" Henceforth, while devoting himself to life, he will think of education as a necessary annoyance for succeeding youths. For him, this life for which he has suffered the affliction of learning will come to be a series of dull, uninteresting, degrading capitulations to the stereotyped pattern of his "set". Within a single decade he will be out of touch with the world of intelligence, or what is worse, he will still be using the intellectual coins of his college days; he will find difficulty in reading serious books; he will have become inured to the jargon of his particular profession and will affect derision for all "highbrows"; he will, in short, have become a typical adult who holds the bag of education—the game of learning having long since slipped by him.

Obviously, extension of the quantity of educational facilities cannot break the circle. Once the belief was current that if only education were free to all intelligence would become the proper tool for managing the affairs of the world. We have gone even further and have made certain levels of education compulsory. But the result has been disappointing; we have succeeded merely in formalizing, mechanizing, educational processes. The spirit and meaning of education cannot be enhanced by addition, by the easy method of giving the same dose to more individuals. If learning is to be revivified, quickened so as to become once more an adventure, we shall have need of new concepts, new motives, new methods; we shall need to experiment with the qualitative aspects of education.

A fresh hope is astir. From many quarters comes the call to a new kind of education with its initial assumption affirming that *education is life*—not a mere preparation for an unknown kind of future living. Consequently all static concepts of education which relegate the learning process to the period of youth are abandoned. The whole of life is learning, therefore education can have no endings. This new venture is called *adult education*—not because it is confined to adults but because adulthood, maturity, defines its limits. The concept is inclusive. The fact that manual workers of Great Britain and farmers of Denmark have conducted the initial experiments which now inspire us does not imply that adult education is designed solely for these classes. No one, probably, needs adult education so much as the college graduate for it is he who makes the most doubtful assumptions concerning the function of learning.

Secondly, education conceived as a process coterminous with life revolves about *non-vocational* ideals. In this world of specialists every one will of necessity learn to do his work, and if education of any variety can assist in this and in the further end of helping the worker to see the meaning of his labor, it will be education of a high order. But adult education more accurately defined begins where vocational education leaves off. Its purpose is to put meaning into the whole of life. Workers, those who perform essential services, will naturally discover more values in continuing education than will those for whom all knowledge is merely decorative or conversational. The possibilities of enriching the activities of labor itself grow less for all workers who manipulate automatic machines. If the good life, the life interfused with meaning and with joy, is to come to these, opportunities for expressing more of the total personality than is called forth by machines will be needed. Their lives will be quickened into creative activities in proportion as they learn to make fruitful use of leisure.

Thirdly, the approach to adult education will be via the route of *situations,* not subjects. Our academic system has grown in reverse order: subjects and teachers constitute the starting-point, students are secondary. In conventional education the student is required to adjust himself to an established curriculum; in adult education the curriculum is built around the student's needs and interests. Every adult person finds himself in specific situations with respect to his work, his recreation, his family-life, his community-life, et cetera—situations which call for adjustments. Adult education begins at this point. Subject-matter is brought into the situation, is put to work, when needed. Texts and teachers play a new and secondary rôle in this type of education; they must give way to the primary importance of the learner. (Indeed, as we shall see later, the teacher of adults becomes also a learner.) The situation-approach to education means that the learning process is at the outset given a setting of reality. Intelligence performs its function in relation to actualities, not abstractions.

In the fourth place, the resource of highest value in adult education is the *learner's experience.* If education is life, then life is also education. Too much of learning consists of vicarious substitution of some one else's experience and knowledge. Psychology is teaching us, however, that we learn what we do, and that therefore all genuine education will keep doing and thinking together. Life becomes rational, meaningful, as we learn to be intelligent about the things we do and the things that happen to us. If we lived sensibly, we should all discover that the attractions of experience increase as we grow older. Correspondingly, we should find cumulative joys in searching out the reasonable meaning of the events in which we play parts. In teaching children it may be necessary to anticipate objective experience by uses of imagination but adult experience is already there waiting to be appropriated. Experience is the adult learner's living textbook.

Authoritative teaching, examinations which preclude original thinking, rigid pedagogical formulæ—all of these have no place in adult education. "Friends educating each other," says Yeaxlee,[2] and perhaps Walt Whitman saw accurately with his fervent democratic vision what the new educational experiment implied when he wrote: "learn from the simple—teach the wise." Small groups of aspiring adults who desire to keep their minds fresh and vigorous; who begin to learn by confronting pertinent situations; who dig down into the reservoirs of their experience before resorting to texts and secondary facts; who are led in the discussion by teachers who are also searchers after wisdom and not oracles: this constitutes the setting for adult education, the modern quest for life's meaning.

But where does one search for life's meaning? If adult education is not to fall into the pitfalls which have vulgarized public education, caution must be exercised in striving for answers to this query. For example, once the assumption is made that human nature is uniform, common and static—that all human beings will find meaning in identical goals, ends or aims—the standardizing process begins: teachers are trained according to orthodox and regulated methods; they teach prescribed subjects to large classes of children who must all pass the same examination; in short, if we accept the standard of uniformity, it follows that we expect, e.g., mathematics, to mean as much to one student as to another. Teaching methods which proceed from this assumption must necessarily become autocratic; if we assume that all values and meanings apply equally to all persons, we may then justify ourselves in using a forcing-method of teaching. On the other hand, if we take for granted that human nature is varied, changing and fluid, we will know that life's meanings are conditioned by the individual. We will then entertain a new respect for personality.

Since the individual personality is not before us we are driven to generalization. In what areas do most people appear to find life's meaning? We have only one pragmatic guide: meaning must reside in the things for which people strive, the goals which they set for themselves, their wants, needs, desires and wishes. Even here our criterion is applicable only to those whose lives are already dedicated to aspirations and ambitions which belong to the higher levels of human achievement.

The adult able to break the habits of slovenly mentality and willing to devote himself seriously to study when study no longer holds forth the lure of pecuniary gain is, one must admit, a personality in whom many negative aims and desires have already been eliminated. Under examination, and viewed from the standpoint of adult education, such personalities seem to want among other things, intelligence, power, self-expression, freedom, creativity, appreciation, enjoyment, fellowship. Or, stated in terms of the Greek ideal, they are searchers after the good life. They want to count for something; they want their experiences to be vivid and meaningful; they want their talents to be utilized; they want to know beauty and joy; and they want all of these realizations of their total personalities to be shared in communities of fellowship. Briefly they want to improve themselves; this is their realistic and primary aim. But they want also to change the social order so that vital personalities will be creating a new environment in which their aspirations may be properly expressed.

II

TO THOSE WHO HAVE FAITH IN INTELLIGENCE

"Thinking cannot be the function of an exclusive caste, still less a function which can be inherited. . . . The first task of intelligence is the establishment of a civilized standard of life."

—C. DELISLE BURNS.

"The most important scientific question of to-day is one that is philosophical: namely, the validity of Science itself as a means of interpreting experience and of acquiring knowledge in respect of what we call the world about us."

—F. G. CROOKSHANK.

"For reason is experimental intelligence, conceived after the pattern of science, and used in the creation of social arts; it has something to do. . . . Intelligence is not something possessed once for all. It is in constant process of forming, and its retention requires constant alertness in observing consequences, an open-minded will to learn and courage in readjustment."

—JOHN DEWEY.

TO THOSE WHO HAVE FAITH IN
INTELLIGENCE

PSYCHOLOGISTS have not yet told us what intelligence is nor how it operates. In fact those psychologists who lay claim to superior wisdom insist that the intellectual process—thinking—has very little to do with the actualities of life. Real adjustment, they affirm, takes place on motor levels; what we are pleased to call thinking is merely a human apology, i.e., a way of rationalizing conduct. Thinking furnishes no energy for acting but merely uses left-over energies for purposes of justifying actions.

We cannot stop here to engage in the current controversy. Before taking sides, it will probably be advisable to view this conflict (which may turn out to be intellectual in character) with perspective. Fashions come and go in scientific as well as in religious dogmas. At least it seems true that intelligence must henceforth take its place with emotion, impulse and neuro-muscular activity—not superior to but coordinate with these other drives and controls of behavior. Reason has not been dethroned but rather democratized. Conduct is best suited to the purposes of the organism which proceeds from harmonious synthesis (integration) of mental, emotional, instinctive and motor levels. Rational conduct is not predominantly intellectual; rather it is conduct in which reason or thought plays a proper part. And rational conduct, no matter what certain

psychologists say, is still the goal of both civilized and
so-called uncivilized people. Thought is somehow mixed
with action and although we can no longer lay claim to
superior capacities for thinking, we are not likely to
abandon the attempt to understand its nature and function. "Man is unwilling to remain in ignorance of the
motives of his own conduct," writes Unamuno, the great
distruster of reason. The more rational of us may add:
he will never be satisfied to leave off trying to understand the meaning of his conduct to himself, to his
environment, to society and to the universe.

If then "intelligence has something to do," what can
its function be? More precisely, in the interests of what
purposes may adults be induced to increase their intelligence? The advantages of *skill*—proficiency in doing
something—are obvious. We must adjust ourselves with
respect to some aspect of skill or be eliminated from
the lists of effective persons in the modern world. The
utilities of *information*—accumulation and retention of
facts—are likewise apparent. And the bulk of our conventional education consists of a pursuit for *knowledge:*
a way of comparing facts and noting their relevancy
within categories. (Intelligence includes these various
aspects of learning, but performs an additional function.)
Intelligence is *reasonable:* seeks out the logic of events; is
objective: seeks the factual reality which lies back of
appearances; is *critical:* views isolated facts and phenomena in relation to *milieux:* presses facts to the level of
relation to other relevant facts; is *tentative:* arrives at

conclusions which are easily revised. These are all significant functions and combine to designate a human being of desirable qualities. To intelligence, however, belongs another and transcendant service.

An intelligent person sees facts, not merely in relation to each other but in relation to himself. Indeed, one of the first marks of intelligence is to recognize that "mental views of the real are aspects of reality." Intelligence then becomes a way of appropriating facts—a way of integrating facts with the total aspects of personality. Only the educated specialist naïvely sees facts as discreet, objective and external units of experience. He speaks of the "laws of nature" as if man's mind were not somehow mixed with the formulation of those laws. Facts, objectively discovered and described in so far as language and mathematical symbols will permit, are empirically important but not nearly so important in an ultimate sense as the method of their discovery and man's disposition of them in the affairs of the world. From the place where the capitalist stands, private ownership of property and the tools of production appears to be conducive to the highest human welfare; to the rationalizing capitalist, acquisition and ownership, and welfare are the pertinent factors of this equation; taken together all three constitute another significant fact. But many persons who are not capitalists reverse this formula; looking out upon the scene from another point of view (i.e., as another organism or personality in a partially different environment) these people see the capitalist and his idea-system as inimical to the highest human welfare. Intelligence steps in with the aim of seeing as many relevant facts as can possibly be revealed; its first discovery will be that both the capitalist and the anti-capitalist have filtered facts through the meshes of their personalities and that consequently they have in reality created two new sets of facts. The most significant aspect of this knowledge is its relation to the interests and values of the respective persons. Again intelligence enters, not to discredit one or the other person but to seek a method for validating the involved interests. Briefly, one of the functions of intelligence—its critical mission—is to give full recognition to the personal equation in all fact-finding and fact-using.

Intelligence is, moreover, experimental. Not all of man's behavior consists of immediate responses to specific stimuli. Our significant acts are those which we "stop to think" about. Whatever concept we may utilize for describing the nature of stimulus, it still remains true that completed responses may be postponed. When we deliberate about two or more courses of action we are interrupting the stimulus, delaying the total response. However short the interval between stimulus and response, here is intellect's opportunity. Intelligence cannot force the organism to do something outside its capacity but it can—either by means of past experience or projected experience—test consequences. It cannot wholly determine action, nor can it foreordain results but it can bring both to the level of awareness or consciousness. The person who knows what he is doing has taken the first step toward intelligent behavior. *The person who knows what he wants to do and why is intelligent.* But he cannot learn the how and the why of conduct by rules and precepts and other persons' experiences; he must experiment on his own behalf. Intelligence is goodness in the sense that one cannot purposefully or positively experience the good unless conscious experimentation in the realm of values accompanies activity. Habitual goodness lacks dynamic qualities—is in fact not goodness in any real or living sense. Our habits can aid us in remaining alive in a changing world but only intelligence can furnish the means for progressive adjustments. Intelligence is not merely the capacity which enables us to profit by experience; it is the function of personality which gives experience its past, present and future meaning. Habits belong to existence, intelligence to living. Life becomes a creative venture in proportion to the amount and quality of intelligence which accompanies conduct.

Psychologically speaking, intelligence is the ability to learn, the capacity to solve problems, to utilize knowledge in evolving, continuing accommodations to changing environments. Intelligent persons are teachable, adaptable. Since life is growth—continuous change—and since environments are never static, new situations are forever arising, and each new situation confronted makes fresh demands upon intelligence. Knowledge and fact are relative to situations. Consequently growing personalities are conditioned by evolving intellectual capacities. We can conceive of a static intelligence only in terms of the paradox of static organisms. Education is the process and experience is the means for achieving evolutionary intelligence. The end is life transfused with meaning.

That the quantity and the quality of intelligence or ability to learn varies with individuals goes without saying. This does not imply, however, that education should be limited to those who happen to possess this capacity in terms of preconceived and arbitrary norms. If we are to make the most effective use of whatever quantity of intelligence is available, we shall need to grant the right of each personality to rise to its own level. This means that increased inventiveness will be required to discover the kind of education which will most effectively meet the needs of varying capacities. Formal educational discipline cannot be accepted as the criterion for ability to learn. The fact that over half the children in our public schools stop at the eighth grade and that only ten to twelve per cent of those who enter high school complete the course may constitute an indictment, not against intelligence, but rather against the formalism of our educational system.

Adult education presents a challenge to static concepts of intelligence, to the standardized limitations of conventional education and to the theory which restricts educational facilities to an intellectual class. Apologists for the status quo in education frequently assert that the great majority of adults are not interested in learning, are not motivated in the direction of continuing education;

if they posessed these incentives, they would, naturally, take advantage of the numerous free educational opportunities provided by public agencies. This argument begs the question and misconceives the problem. We shall never know how many adults desire intelligence regarding themselves and the world in which they live until education once more escapes the patterns of conformity. Adult education is an attempt to discover a new method and create a new incentive for learning; its implications are qualitative, not quantitative. Adult learners are precisely those whose intellectual aspirations are least likely to be aroused by the rigid, uncompromising requirements of authoritative, conventionalized institutions of learning.

III

WITH RESPECT TO THE USE OF POWER

"We can have power only over ourselves. . . . This kind of power, power-with, is what democracy should mean in politics or industry, but as we have not taken the means to get a genuine power, pseudo-power has leapt into the saddle."

—M. P. Follett.

"Obviously the appeal to force can only show who is strong, not who is wrong."

—M. C. Otto.

WITH RESPECT TO THE USE OF
POWER

"KNOWLEDGE and human power," said Francis Bacon, "are synonymous, since the ignorance of the cause frustrates the effect." Man feels himself propelled, motivated, controlled by forces external to himself. When the mood of pessimism overtakes him he comes to believe that the ultimate meaning of life is restricted to these involuntary effects which constitute his behavior and which proceed from unknown causes. But never "in our dejection do we sink" beyond the sight of hope; melancholia is temporary. Human nature is predisposed to optimism. We never wholly abandon the struggle to become what Disraeli thought us to be; namely, the "instruments who create circumstances".

Science, curiously enough, furnishes grounds for both our expectations and illusions. Scientific discoveries present cumulative evidence of our dependence upon inexorable natural laws, but it is likewise the scientist who teaches us that "the earth yields; step by step death itself gives ground; and shall we think of the stars only to fear them and to read our fate in them?" [3] Indeed, Western Civilization has become so far imbued with scientific elation that we all tend to agree with Singer in defining progress as "the measure of man's coöperation with man in the conquest of nature".[4] Our world is dynamic precisely because of this faith in man's capacity to direct his destiny. And, we still believe with Bacon that the power which gives man this assurance within the order of nature is his capacity for knowledge. We obey his injunction "to begin to form an acquaintance with things" with the accompanying confidence that our knowledge *of* will lead to control *over* the objects of our environment. Our achievements have been prodigious. We can, by taking thought, change into man's servants forces once inimical to his welfare; we can equip the white man for life in the tropics although it is not "natural" that he should live there; we can design machines which do the work of men; we are able to shrink distances and defy time; in short, we can by the applications of science alter, transform the natural environment. Human beings exercise *power over* nature.

Limits to this exercise of power are obvious. Man succeeds in accommodating himself and his purposes to the order of nature by means of adjustments *to* and *with,* not against natural processes. Human nature is itself a part of the order of nature and cannot escape its naturalness. We are free and independent only insofar as freedom and independence are aspects of organic activity in a changing environment. The power which we exert over natural forces is germane, not external to nature's domain. We build false hopes when, as Bukharin says, we enter the "confusion between the *feeling* of independence, and real *objective* independence.[5] Nevertheless, our power over nature, such as it is, has been achieved by intellectual processes. Scientific method is a discovery, if not an invention, of man's mind. Moreover, this power which utilizes natural forces has come to be also the most potent manipulator of our lives. Inhabitants of the modern world must somehow effect an adjustment between the knowledge of nature (science) and their thinking. We are all subject to this power; we should all also so far as possible understand its significance. The hiatus between a life dominated increasingly by science and a life rationalized in terms of unscientific or anti-scientific thought represents one of the most appalling deficiencies of our civilization. The remedy does not lie in simply adding more scientific subjects to school curricula. Only by sustained continuous intellectual effort can we keep abreast of our science and its ensuing power over our lives. If we stop for ever so brief a time, dynamic science will leap ahead of our comprehension. Adult education presumes, then, to serve as one of the means by which the mind may be kept fresh for the assimilation of that knowledge which is synonymous with power.

The urge to power is a many-faceted motivation for our behavior. We desire power over nature and, alas, many of us also strive for power over other human beings. Indeed, during the rise of capitalism power over natural resources and forces has frequently been appropriated solely as a means for accumulating wealth; and wealth is, for us at least, the symbol of power over others. The

"Great Society" has come to be a vast network of power-groups, each vying with the other for supremacy. Nationalism and imperialism are merely outward manifestations of this "pseudo-power" which degrades us all; beneath these more glamorous units lies the pervading economic structure of our civilization based upon a doubtful competitive ethic and avowedly designed to benefit the crafty, the strong and the truculent. Industrial organization evolves steadily into a complex of separatist groups—financiers, employers, stockholders, workers, consumers—each of which learns in time to conceive of its interests in terms of ultimate opposition to the interests of the others. The system can operate only under the dispensation of discontinuous truces. Warfare is the rule of the game.

Nothing positive results from mere shifts of power; this is the lesson which labor movements need to learn. If half the time devoted to revolutionary propaganda could be directed toward refining the aspirations of workers, a real transformation would sooner or later take place. Premature workers' control may, indeed, do nothing more than accentuate old evils: the desire to do unto others what they have been accustomed to do unto us is an invariable by-product of sudden power-exchanges. If workers bring into industrial control nothing better in the way of a philosophy of power than the present concept of capitalists and employers, the net gain will be zero. We stand in need of a revolution of the mind—not a mere exchange of power-groups—before an economic revolution can transform industry into a coöperative enterprise, before "power *over*" is transposed into "power *with*" in industry. Labor will inject a new and creative element into the control of economic forces when workers are actuated by cleaner motives, sharper intellectual insights and finer wills. In the meantime, labor's future strategy will, without doubt, depart gradually from its struggle-technique, that is, from the irrational method of attempting to prove who is wrong by demonstrating who is strong. The trade union of the future will be a creating, not merely a fighting, organization. This implies, obviously, a transformation of trade union habits, habits which are now so deeply imbedded in the behavior-patterns of the older leaders that they will find it difficult if not impossible to make the adjustment. Workers' education, already the most vital sector of the adult education movement, forecasts a new phase of industrial readjustment: the displacement of the use of force by the use of intelligence. Through the process will come new accessions of power for the worker, but if his education results in real intelligence as distinguished from mere mental cunning, it will be power which leads to new concurrences and integrations, not to the renewal of old frictions. Labor will come into its own when workers discover better motives for production and finer meanings for life.

We desire, if we are normal human beings, power over our environments, over the mechanized forces which surround us, over the factors which control our labors: power, that is, over the external objects and energies with respect to which our significant conduct is conditioned. We refuse to acknowledge ourselves "creatures of circumstances"; if there is for us a potential area of choice, we mean to find it. And so we go forth with our scientific tools and technologies to conquer nature, to develop ever-increasing resources of power. Likewise, some set forth to learn the methods for conquering people, confident also that power vested in themselves will validate the assumption that men shape events. Success in both spheres is ours: man with his little but restless brain has transfigured the face of the earth and dictators now rule in seven nations. We are capable of developing sufficient intelligence to secure at least partial control over things and we know how to govern people by coercion. But we have thus far failed completely in devising intelligent procedures for socializing power. We still stumble along in the sphere of human relations with no guide other than the wornout, discredited, cruel presumption that power is achieved by victory over another person or group: that *my* advantage must mean *your* disability; that efficacy for *me* can exist only through *your* disqualification.

No human being can safely be trusted with power until he has learned how to exercise power over himself. We are slowly coming to see that all "power-grabbers" and dictators who reach out for unusual power are in reality compensating for inner deficiencies of their personalities. To wish for power is thoroughly normal; to want power in order to make myself great while you are made small is abnormal. Again a problem, the solution of which depends upon an extension of intelligence, confronts us—one that cannot be transferred to the younger generation. Children do not, it is true, inherit dispositions to power over others; they acquire this urge by watching their elders. They could, by proper educational stimulus, be conditioned for more wholesome social relationships. But the momentous and necessary adjustment which all children must soon or late attack is accommodation to the adult world with its complex of habits, customs, *mores* and traditions. If these compulsions of the adult process are too rigid, no genuine adjustment can take place, only capitulation and compromise. Youth, fluid, generous and adventurous, attempting to adapt its life to adulthood which is rigid, competitive and contemptuous—this is the perfect equation, the quotient of which is endless and useless conflicts, subterfuge and dishonesty. Somehow we must learn to cleanse the dreams of old men so that the visions seen by young men will not turn into bitterness. "Whoso neglects learning in his youth, loses the past and is dead for the future" and Euripides might have added: whoso neglects learning in old age contaminates the present.

Adults who once more venture forth on the pathway of learning will do well to give attention to Bacon's advice; knowledge is surely one of the chief aspects of power. And, he who would be at home in the modern world will need to "form an acquaintance with things".

If, however, he is content to remain on this level, he will fall short of the genuine power which is wisdom. To find the clew for educational effort which includes knowledge of the self he will need to go beyond Bacon, perhaps to the Greeks. "Know thyself" taught Socrates. "Learning is ever in the freshness of its youth, even for the old," said Æschylus.

IV

IN VIEW OF THE NEED FOR SELF-EXPRESSION

"O to be self-balanced for contingencies."

—WALT WHITMAN.

"For in both the life of man and the life of nature, individuality remains the irreducible surd."

—HORACE KALLEN.

IN VIEW OF THE NEED FOR
SELF-EXPRESSION

INTELLIGENCE is consciousness in action—behavior with a purpose. The person who is vividly aware of his activity as well as the goal toward which the activity is directed becomes conscious of both his powers and limitations. We evaluate a personality by two generalized questions: What constitutes the validity of his goals? And, is his behavior effective with respect to his chosen goals or ends? If we disapprove of his ends, we will naturally condemn both his ends and means. On the other hand, if we sanction his ends but suspect his means, we will regard him as a deficient personality but capable of being educated. Vocational education is designed to equip students with the proper means for arriving at their selected goals. Adult education goes beyond the means and demands new sanctions, new vindications of ends.

In the previous chapter we have dealt with power— one of the ends or goals for which people strive. Power itself, that is, directive energy, is not to be condemned but we need to ask pertinent questions regarding the manner of its use. Power-over, even when exercised by the most benevolent of despots, invariably debases both those who command and those who obey. Any force, in fact, which by its function deprives those concerned

[33]

from participation and choice belittles and degrades their personalities. The king, dictator, employer or teacher who does things for others which they might have accomplished for themselves thereby weakens the capacity and worth of citizens, workers and students. Personality has functions which, if not brought into action, disintegrate. A functional personality is hence one which realizes its powers, that is, somehow gets itself expressed. Therefore only those selves which have been self-discovered can get realized, expressed. Knowledge of the self discloses what the self is capable of expressing.

In the modern world of specialism only a small sector of personality is set into motion through vocational activities. We all tend to become specialists—which means that we all tend to become fractional personalities. This involves not merely an immediate loss to ourselves— a shrinking of our personalities—but in addition is a great loss to the world since we cannot have broad and generous societies composed of narrow and limited citizens. Educators, aware of the responsibility of the school to the child's evolving self, have proposed innumerable experiments for encouraging self-expression on the part of beginning pupils. Some schools—still too few in number—base their entire approach to the education of the child upon methods of discovering latent interests, urges to self-expression. These experimental efforts are to be encouraged. Nevertheless, the child reared in an educational atmosphere of self-expression will be rudely shocked to find that he has somehow to

make his way in a community which regards self-expression as an aspect of abnormality—a community which
asks for but one of the functions of the multiple self.
Again we see that a society of articulate selves will never
be created by youth; the task belongs to those adults who
still retain sufficient courage to refuse social representation on the basis of fragmentary personality.

Adults who make bold to revive the once vivid interests
of their total personalities will need to submit themselves
to a process of *reëducation*. Their habit-systems will resist;
the vocational organization in which they labor will
continue its demand for specialized, partial functions;
they will need to be motivated by ends which are either
exterior or in opposition to the incentives which lead to
pecuniary success. The whole of these environmental
resistances tends to tempt the organism toward conformity; why go through the bothersome toil of reëducating
my habits if the present ones serve to keep me alive,
well-fed, well-clothed and well-housed? Most Americans
will probably find no satisfactory answer to this argument
so long as our unique prosperity endures. The eye of
the needle is forever small for those tempted into self-
indulgence by wealth. Some, however, are coming to
believe with William James that "the squalid cash interpretation put on the word success is our national disease."
They also look upon some of our absurd educational
assumptions as symptoms of this same illness: we could
not have developed such barren maturity, such lack of
intellectual interest in adults, had we not first of all

misconceived our goals. "... if life is to be lived not only, but won to excellency," we shall do well to listen to these few who point out to us the impossibility of building a wholesome society out of partially starved personalities.

What then are intelligent personalities to express, give forth? First of all: individuality, uniqueness, difference. Personality is in essence a synthesis of the bodily and mental functions acting in relation to environment. Such synthesis can never be the same in two organisms. Individuality is the qualitative relation between elements of personality. We live and move in a social environment but we have our being within the organic unity of particularized selves. Difference is the base of personal integrity. Only the unintelligent fear what differs from themselves. We should, if we were bravely intelligent, beg individuals to give us their difference, not their sameness. Nothing exciting can happen in a world of uniformities and homogeneities. Divergence is the factor which induces a life of succeeding contingencies— a life, that is, in which individual conduct is of import.[6]

Communities on the road toward intelligence recognize "that creation comes from the impact of diversities"[7] but thus far the privileges of freely expressing individual difference have been restricted mainly to artists and the extremely wealthy. The latter are exempted from the monotonies, not because society expects them to develop productive gifts, but merely because our inverted standards make wealth and privilege synonymous. Artists justify their freedom by their works. Great art is always an expression of a released personality. And, life is not the least of arts. Persons in fiction or life called "characters" are those who have frankly expressed their singular traits—those who have resisted the pattern of conformity. In this sense we can achieve character solely by expressing what is peculiar to ourselves. Many persons attain this level of zestful living by virtue of native gifts; others need to fortify themselves against conventional routine through the exercise of intelligence. We lose our timidity and gain the courage of self in proportion to our knowledge of what life is about. Adults who have learned to respect those values which can arise through individual expression alone already live in the land where life's meaning may be discovered.

Personalities, conscious of their powers and appreciative of their individualities, will inevitably feel the urge to participate in public affairs; they will wish for some share in creating the environment which furnishes the stimulating background for their lives. Mere *feeling* of difference may lead to idiosyncrasy; differences which do not get themselves realized in action may readily become negative regrets and frustrations. Once we lose the sense of active, directive participation in affairs, we sink to the level of inaction, or what is worse, silent opposition. Politics and industry, for example, provide unusual opportunities for self-expression to those who have the power to manipulate. The citizen, however, progressively loses interest in government, and the worker grows apathetic over the efficiency of industry because each in his sphere feels that governing and managing make no use of his personal gifts. Merely voting, that is, counting each personality as one, does not, as Miss Follett [8] has demonstrated, reach to the bottom of the difficulty. We have, indeed, become weary of being counted; we want to count for something.

If we are to create opportunities which will call forth contributory personalities, small beginnings in the realm of the manageable will bring more rapid progress than attempts at reforming such vast and unwieldy units as industry and the state. Each of us is capable of bringing intelligent influence to bear somewhere—in home, neighborhood, community, trade union, coöperative society, trade association, et cetera. Adult education specifically aims to train individuals for a more fruitful participation in those smaller collective units which do so much to mold significant experience. All education worthy of the name aspires to become art rather than skill, and adult education is devoted to the task of training individuals in "the art of transmuting . . . experience into influence"; [9] the adult learner becomes *"a spokesman for ideas"*—ideas which represent his personality and which constitute his peculiar contribution to life. We need, then, to be educated for self-expression because individuality is the most precious gift we have to bring to the world—and further, because the personal self can never be adequately represented by proxy. Personality becomes dynamic in terms of intelligent self-expression.

One of the aspects of diversity in human beings which conventional education too frequently overlooks is the variety of recreational or enjoyable experiences. Recreation, like most other elements in modern life, tends to become stereotyped, standardized. We are all supposed to enjoy baseball; and if we are college students, football and dancing; if club members, auction bridge or golf; et cetera, et cetera. The hours of play, alas, come to be also compelling hours. But, this is a denial of the very essence of play. Necessity may lead us to capitulate to machine-industry with its consequent limitations of movement and self-expression, but what compulsion exists to make you pretend to enjoy the same pleasures which fascinate me? Play is nothing but exercise if it does not permit the free expression of personal inclination, individual enjoyment. Recreation should above all else be movements of freedom, response which calls into play the total personality, activity of grace, release, gladness. Here, if anywhere, individual choice must be supreme, else even in play we learn to abandon personal integrity and worth. Adult educators will be alert to discover what activities give joy to particular students; they will be on the watch to uncover temperamental hobbies, pursuits which may seem ludicrous to others but which to the doer bring peculiar satisfactions. Indeed, adult education will have justified itself if it does nothing more than make adults happier in their hours of leisure. Grown-up moderns are pathetic precisely because they know how to achieve everything save pure delight for its own sake.

Even in games, the end—victory—and not the process is dominant. When my thought is upon adult education memory invariably recalls the Danish farmer who spent his leisure hours painting scenes of his farm and neighborhood. One of the canvases—showing a typical Danish rural scene—which adorned his modest home pleased me so much that I offered to purchase it; he not only refused the bargain but severely reprimanded me for presuming to place a pecuniary valuation upon the product of his recreation. Necessity compelled him to be a farmer but he had all his life dreamed of expressing himself in art. He was a most efficient farmer but farming did not bring into play the whole of his personality. A young German instructor in his local folk-school (school for adults) had released in him this aspiration to paint and had aided him toward skill; now at the age of fifty he finds felicity in painting pictures which express something of his personality—something which necessary work could never have called forth. Even this activity did not exhaust his individual resources: I recall a memorable night spent in his home when the topic of discussion was the poetry of Walt Whitman—the American who knew how to "let himself go free". He called our Walt "the Danish farmer's poet" and shame taunts me still when I think of all he found in Whitman's poems—all that had escaped me.

V

FOR THOSE WHO REQUIRE
FREEDOM

". . . and a man is free in whom all capacities for activity and enjoyment flow out to the extent of their strength. . . . It has been assumed that freedom means the absence of limitation, which is correct but misleading; for it explains by a negative, and has therefore led to the absurdities of individualism . . . the value of freedom lies in the original impulse, and not in the absence of an obstacle."

—C. Delisle Burns.

"Learning does not liberate men from superstition when their souls are cowed or perplexed."

—George Santayana.

FOR THOSE WHO REQUIRE FREEDOM

THE times are not attuned for a sympathetic reception of ideas on freedom. If John Stuart Mill's *Essay on Liberty* were to be given to the contemporary public for the first time, it would surely fall upon barren ground. We now think of power and freedom in Machiavellian terms: we continue to talk about freedom while we acquire power for its suppression. And all because we have persistently misconceived the nature of liberty!

Our error may be traced in at least three directions: (a) freedom was thought of in terms of absence of control—a purely negative concept; (b) freedom was associated with the spurious theological doctrine of free will; (c) all practical means for achieving freedom were vitiated by false separations of inseparable unities —individual versus society, citizen versus state, will versus instinct, et cetera. We have, in short, consistently sought to be free *from* things which appeared as obstacles: Rousseau sought liberation from civilization, Jonathan Edwards strove to endow human nature with a will which would free him from all bodily and wordly compulsions, and John Stuart Mill envisaged individuals freed from the constraints of public opinion. The *naïveté* of these negative strivings for freedom are revealed the moment we attempt to visualize an individual cut off from the civilization of his time, endowed with a will

[43]

dissociated from his body, and existing in a society which allows only *his* opinions to count. We then begin to see that human beings can never be free *from* anything save in a most superficial sense; we cannot be parts of a natural universe, a civilization and a society and at the same time also be separated from these wholes of which we are parts. There is no "One and the Many,"—merely many ones in the one. The doctrine of freedom *from* is not merely static and negative; it is also irrational and harmful. The personality on the way toward disintegration strives to be free from realities; or, perhaps it is more correct to say that the attempt to escape realities is the first indication of a disintegrating personality. Only the insane complete the process.

Human nature cannot violate nature. We exist within a natural environment and all our behavior is a response to, a function of, the multitudinous stimuli which arise either within or without our bodies and operate according to natural laws which we dimly understand. Stimuli or causes are somehow related to responses or effects in us as well as in the universe of which we are parts. We can therefore be free only within the scheme of nature. Successful human adjustment is never wholly *to* or *against* nature, but always partially *with;* we cannot be free *from* ourselves or the natural objects which surround us, and consequently the only freedom worth talking about is *freedom-with.*

The intelligent alone are free for only by knowing what it is we can be free *with,* can we find freedom at all. "Nothing," writes Arthur Ponsonby, "is more pathetic than the confidence with which humanity believes it can master vast forces which are quite obviously beyond human regulation." Nothing, perhaps, save the brutality, waste and suffering which result because man despairs of mastering the minute forces which are obviously within his control. Man is, fortunately or otherwise, equipped with a so-called higher brain center, the cortex, which enables him, unlike other animals, to react to his environment with a certain degree of choice or freedom; he is less dependent upon instinctive responses. "It is the function of the cortex which enables man to indulge in reflective thought, and so acquire his great ascendancy over the animals." [10] Higher mental processes emerge by virtue of the cortical functions of association, correlation and integration. Voluntary conduct is, then, not an inversion of natural processes but rather a new combination of factors. The manner in which these new emergents of behavior arise has been explained by Lloyd Morgan,[11] John Dewey,[12] Edwin Holt,[13] M. P. Follett,[14] R. G. Gordon[15] and others and need not be further elaborated here. For present purposes it is sufficient to know that an area of relative freedom of thought-action exists for man and that the hypothesis upon which this assumption rests is of supreme importance to education.

We are free in proportion to the number of things we can create (not *de novo* out of nothing) or invent by utilizing what we already have. We do not discard old patterns of behavior in favor of new: we combine old ones with the result that new patterns emerge. Thus inventions on the physical or mechanical level are always recombinations of existing elements. And we now know by better means than mere analogy that the process of intellectual integration is similar. Freedom is an achievement, not a gift. We do not acquire freedom—we grow into freedom. Alas, many of us are still wistful, disappointed seekers. "He was always," writes Walter Pater, of Watteau, "a seeker after something in the world that is there in no satisfying measure, or not at all." And, many of us still go groping about in the vain hope that freedom may be *found* or bought by some political or legal expedient.

The first step toward liberation is taken when an individual begins to understand what inhibits, frustrates, subjugates him. We learn to be free when we know what we desire freedom for and what stands in the way of our desire. Psycho-therapy has taught us that the first look must be within, not without. Most of the barriers to freedom have been self-constructed, self-induced. We already know, empirically at least, that many of our desires and wishes are validated and many obstacles dissolved by means of bringing our submerged conflicts to the level of consciousness. In one sense, freedom is conscious conduct. The psycho-therapeutic specialist does not "cure" his patient; he merely assists the patient in learning the methods of self-recovery. And the method is self-knowledge.

In another sense we become free when we discover the limitations and extent of our capacities. Much of the discontent among adults is due to fruitless striving after impractical or impossible objectives. We set Utopian goals, impossible targets, and then sink into thralldom because our Utopias never arrive and our shots all miss the mark. We suffer the bitterness of impotency because we have all along striven for an ideal beyond our capacities. On the other hand, if we take life as it is and begin our experimentations in behavior in terms of possible and manageable ideals, we will always be conscious of growth and renewal. We can save ourselves from furtive fantasy only by keeping our aims within the area of the real and the possible. Not that all adults should begin their reëducation by submitting to intelligence tests, forthwith to order their future lives on the basis of their limitations —a process patently stultifying and inimical to growth. On the contrary, the implication is that "one change always leaves a babbitting on which another can be built" —that we increase our capacities by means of achievements which are now possible. Limits of freedom are reached only when we have exhausted all of the possibilities within grasp of growing capacities. "Every important satisfaction of an old want creates a new one," says Dewey,[16] and so every attainment in the ordering of our conscious conduct gives rise to new possibilities.

Attention to the sources of freedom which lie within human personality should not close our eyes to the fact that many of the forces which enslave us are environmental. In a static environment, individuals cannot change in the direction of freedom. We want freedom because we believe it will increase our happiness but sooner or later we are sure to discover that individuals cannot be free in a feudal society. We need continuing education in order to learn awareness of ourselves as behaving organisms but we also need more knowledge concerning those external factors of which our behavior is a constant function. The aim should be, not to teach adult students that, e.g., a subject called economics exists and needs to be studied, but rather that there are economic factors in his total situations and that he must somehow come to know how to deal with these if his total situations are to emerge as progressive sequences of living. The old debate over environment versus heredity (or organism) has lost its meaning now that we have come to see that organism-environment are two interacting parts of a unified equation. We can progress not by giving attention to either organism or environment, but to both and in relation to each other. Propaganda organizations will of course make use of adult education as a means to achieve their preconceived environmental ends—which, unhappily, will lead to further illusions concerning education. The doctrinaire revolutionist who sees the problem of freedom in terms of a binding environment and an enslaving social and economic order will naturally seek education as a force to release him and his fellow-believers; he will, indeed, construct a faith in the possibility of altering his entire life *after* the revolution which changes the social order. This point of view is easily condemned on theoretic grounds, but even educators ought not to lose sight of the fact that revolutions are occasionnaly necessary. We may, for example, so far exaggerate the incentives and motives which are derived from capitalism and profit-production as to cause the entire educational system to become a direct response to this system and to lead to its further emphasis. At present the majority of college graduates in the United States probably leave college with increased rather than with diminished profit motives. At any rate, they do very little either as critics or experimenters to create new motives. If this system, both on its economic and educational sides, becomes too rigid and too oppressive and incapable of sincere self-criticism, nothing short of violent revolution will suffice to change its direction. But if adults approach education with the end-in-view that their new knowledge is to be the instrument of a probable future revolution, they will almost certainly defeat the very purposes of learning. Revolutions are essential only when the true learning process has broken down, failed. We revolt when we can no longer think or when we are assured that thinking has lost its efficacy. Revolution is the last resort of a society which has lost faith in intelligence.

The egotist is slave to his own limitations; the freedom which he verbally affirms is in essence an artificial separation of himself from others. "I listened for the echo," says Nietzsche's *Disappointed One,* "and I heard only praise." Why disappointed? Because self-praise feeds upon itself, is absurd since it has no reliable reference and leads to void. The sense of freedom arrives when we become sufficiently intelligent to face both ourselves and our environments critically, that is, with the feeling that both may be projected as evolutions. Freedom is a creative relatedness between personality and the manageable aspects of the universe. Since nothing possesses meaning save in relation to something else, it follows that freedom becomes significant when viewed in relation to its proper references. To be free from bondage is preliminary; dynamic freedom stirs the personality in the direction of radical, causative, originative activity. The function of freedom is to create.

In summary, those individuals are free who know their powers and capacities as well as their limitations; who seek a way of life which utilizes their total personalities; who aim to alter their conduct in relation to a changing environment in which they are conscious of being active agents. Each of these components of freedom is dependent upon a degree of intelligence and is realizable in terms of education. Both the amount of intelligence and learning essential for free self-expression varies with individuals. Freedom can never be absolute. None of us is self-determined. Self is relative to other selves and to the inclusive environment. We live in freedom when we are conscious of a degree of self-direction proportionate to our capacities.

VI

FOR THOSE WHO WOULD CREATE

"The common problem, yours, mine, everyone's,
  Is—not to fancy what were fair in life
  Provided it could be—but, finding first
  What may be, then find how to make it fair
  Up to our means;"

—Quoted by HARRY SNELL.

"Only if to each moment of life there is vividly present the sense that it is a moment of creation, and equally present a satisfaction in the vision of what is to be created, can the moment be a joyous one."

—EDGAR A. SINGER.

FOR THOSE WHO WOULD CREATE

INTELLIGENCE for power, power for self-expression, and self expression in a context of relative freedom: this is the sequence which leads to creative living. But, what are we to create? What is the meaning of power, self-expression and freedom with respect to the total complex of life? Each of these aspects of progressive personalities isolated and left standing by itself becomes a symbol of abnormality: the over-intelligent become intellectual at the expense of social usefulness; those who concentrate on self-expression for its own sake evolve toward egotism; those who accumulate power without full recognition of its social nature turn out to be dictators and arbitrary masters who must have their slaves; and those who seek to make freedom an absolutist goal come ultimately to be detached, baulked cynics.

Intelligence, power, self-expression and freedom come to have meaning only when we see them as coöperating parts of a functioning whole: the integrated personality. Only the intelligent can have justifiable power; only those conscious of power, inner resources, can achieve adequate self-expression; and, in the end, only the free can create. Consequently, the adult learner who sets forth to educate himself in terms of any single objective will defeat his ends. We do not, as learners, first secure intelligence, next power, then self-expression, and last freedom. On the contrary, we experience these aspects of

[53]

personality as concurrences, as forces which flow into each other at moments of creativity.

Most normal youths feel at some time or other during the untamed years a distinct urge toward creativeness. Which of us has not brought his imaginary invention, poem, novel, drama, painting to the red glow of half-realization in some sublime moment of aspiration? And who from the plane of compelling maturity has not looked backward with bitterness upon the unrealized dream? In a poignant dialogue between father and son at commencement time, the elder speaks:

"Has college standardized you as it did your father; has it stood you in a mold, made conventional and neat and proper your ideas of life; or has there come from somewhere some thought or hope of something different, more true, more genuine, more joyful, if you want to put it that way, than what you and I and the alumni of all our universities, for the most part, have come to regard as the safe and sane norm of excellence, a tailor-made pattern, all alike, and so deadly dull that all life has departed from it? . . . Forgive me. Your father, you see, was momentarily living old days over again, or what might have been old days had things been otherwise. He is well along in years, you know; his clothes fit well; he is not worried about the grocer's bill nor his insurance payment; he has never been blackballed at a club nor sneered at in the street, nor driven out of town, nor tarred and feathered or anything else exciting. He was just wondering if he hadn't missed something." [17]

And, this is the tragedy of modern life: even those who win the badge of what we call success find themselves defeated at maturity; defeated because their personalities have become sterile, uncreative. To me nothing is more pitiful than the frantic efforts of art-collecting on the part of the aged rich—the mere urge to collect being so patently a compensation for the failure to create. The newly rich man who purchased books by the yard for his expensive new library and selected them on the basis of the color of bindings represents the tragic absurdity of an inverted culture.

Adult education presumes that the creative spark may be kept alive throughout life, and moreover, that it may be rekindled in those adults who are willing to devote a portion of their energies to the process of becoming intelligent. Once more it becomes necessary to propose inclusive definitions: if life is learning and learning is life, then creativeness is a possibility in all spheres of activity to which significance is attached. The verb "to create" has too long remained the private possession of those who call themselves artists. Life is also one of the creative arts, else its ultimate meaning is boredom. A well-organized and adequately expressed life deserves to be called beautiful no less than a well-conceived statue. Aesthetics suffers by reason of its artificial isolation, its exclusiveness. Beauty is not discovered solely by contemplation of beautiful objects; beauty is experiencing.

Indeed, passive contemplation of beauty in objects or in terms of abstract conceptions may, and often does, become a hindrance to the process of bringing forth active participations in creative experiences. The æsthete invariably degenerates to the level of impotency. He may perceive beauty but is rarely capable of translating his perceptions in terms of the whole of life. To him beauty is not merely an experience to be enjoyed but forever remains a goddess to be worshiped.

Our Danish farmer who painted pictures of genuine quality in his hours of leisure was in addition an active participator in a creative society. He was a member of some dozen or more coöperative associations: social inventions which performed economic services so efficiently that much of his energy could be utilized in the pursuit of higher ends. Moreover, he did not travel to Venice to paint the formal beauties of St. Marks; he found his subjects on his farmstead and in his neighborhood. Consequently his indigenous art exerted a profound influence upon his total life and the life of his community as well. Between life and art no artificial demarcation was erected and all the cant about art and beauty which makes the conversations of æsthetes so superficial was absent. He talked less about art because he lived artistically.

Whenever we are presented with the opportunity of bringing beauty out of ugliness, harmony out of conflict, good-will out of hatred, potency out of sterility, intelligence out of ignorance, in short, whenever it becomes possible to add a new quality to experience, we stand in the presence of creation. The moment may come unforeseen, and therefore we ought always to face life in a creative mood. We may be called on the morrow to a committee-meeting of our fellows to discuss problems of importance. If we enter the discussion with our minds riveted to a preconceived conclusion, the creative spirit will depart from our deliberations; we will come out as we went in, unchanged and unaffected by what might have been a lively coöperative venture. On the next day an issue of state impends; the formalists of politics have prejudged the case by stating its form in terms of opposites, mutually-exclusive factors; if we merely choose one or the other of these prearranged solutions, we express merely the least common denominator of our personalities, not our best. Or, if we are trade unionists who imagine that our best chances of success lie in the use of force rather than in intelligence, our efforts will lead to successive restatements and reformulations of static situations. On the other hand, if we faced every conflict in life as an opportunity for creativeness, most of the drabness, futility and wastefulness of human intercourse could be transmuted into exciting adventures.

We have already learned in part that we must allow those who wish to be called specialists in art a degree of freedom which is not common to all. By their ensuing creativeness, artists and geniuses justify the liberties we permit them. And, we shall eventually learn that a similar sort of freedom must be granted to those who wish to create new ways of life—new industrial, social, economic, educational, international experiments. If living too is to become one of the creative arts, we must discover solvents for those hard partitions which separate life into compartments. We cannot expect youth to reform our rigid institutions if their education proceeds from adult sources and their personalities have to find expression in a context of adult compulsions. The rigidities of adulthood need loosening before anything creative can happen in the sphere of social control. And we need not await the tide of numbers: a small group of adults in a single community seriously concerned about the values of creative living is sufficient to alter the quality of the total community process.

The creative mood is more than an attitude of expectancy. Many persons approach adulthood with Micawber-like confidence in the coming event, the glorious adventure which is bound to happen *to* them, and cumulatively lose capacity to achieve; their imaginative projections lead to such exaggerated introspections and fantasies that they can compensate for their failure to create only by further and more extravagant conceits. In the end they either reach absurd limits of ineffectiveness or drop suddenly to the level of cynicism and despair. Creativeness is always futuristic, anticipatory, but its futurism emanates from the plane of actuality; its "impossibles" are distillations from "possibles." Creativeness is intrinsic and seems fortuitous merely because we fail to see all of the relations between the creator and the combining factors of his creation. Further, creativeness is less dependent upon its ends than its means; the creative process, not the created object, is of supreme importance. We are not all equipped by temperament, organic integration or environmental surroundings to produce works of art but we can all live artistically.

VII

TO THOSE WHO APPRECIATE

"Annette, who instinctively loved the light, had sought for it where she could, in those university studies which in her set were regarded as pretentious. But the light she had found there had been much filtered; it was the light of lecture-rooms and libraries, refracted, never direct."

—ROMAIN ROLLAND.

"Integrating art and life would mean so transforming life that the purposes of art become the purposes of life as well."

—LEO STEIN.

"For art fixes those standards of enjoyment and appreciation with which other things are compared; it selects the objects of future desires; it stimulates effort."

—JOHN DEWEY.

TO THOSE WHO APPRECIATE

THE classic tradition in art is one of the many hurdles which adult learners must jump before they can participate freely and creatively in cultural enjoyments. Nothing so effectively dampens the ardors of appreciation as to told by some formalist that the object being appreciated is unworthy, in bad taste. The proper retort is, of course, *Whose* taste? To this the conventionalist can only reply, Mine—which obviously answers nothing. Our mentor can thereupon refer us to the specimens from which his standards are derived and if he happens to be a professional teacher of art, he will persist until we succumb to Philistinism and pretend to enjoy what he enjoys. But enjoyment is not simulation, reference to patterns and specimens, imitative worship; the essence of enjoyment is critical appreciation. And to appreciate is to assimilate, to appropriate, to make one's own. Appreciation is creative, not passive. But one valid reference for artistic standards exists, namely, the individual who appreciates, enjoys. Every attempt to formulate collective norms must fail by reason of individual variations. My enjoyment can be your enjoyment only in terms of superficial agreements; beneath these common factors lies the uniquences which is forever yours or mine. Enjoyment can never be mutual because those who enjoy are separate organisms living in differing relations of time and space. Moreover, the function of enjoying is derived from organic integrations

[63]

which may be similar but never identical. The foregoing does not imply that enjoyments cannot be shared. Indeed, it may be justifiable to believe that language, communication itself, arose out of the compulsions to share enjoyments as well as dangers. All of us, save the misanthropic and the snobbish, feel the urge to accelerate and intensify our enjoyments by social means, but we succeed merely in stimulating others to their enjoyment. In the search for appreciative and enjoyable experience each goes his way alone. What is enjoyed registers itself ultimately within a psycho-physical process which is the foundation of individual personality. The shareable portions are new social products which may be called *our* enjoyments in the sense that they are derivatives of discreet individual enjoyments.

Adult education, wherever it endures long enough to pass through the "bread and butter" stage, invariably evolves toward cultural ends. In Denmark, Germany *

---

* EDITOR'S NOTE: Lindeman has reference to the relatively liberal post World War I developments in Germany under the Weimar Republic. Of this era Abraham Flexner could write "Prior to the War, the demand for adult education, growing with the increase in the number and influence of the Social Democrats, was unsatisfactorily met, partly by associations of workingmen, which offered one-sided and superficial instruction, partly by the universities, whose professors, out of touch with the workingman, talked over his head. The present movement, directed under the terms of the Weimar Constitution by the Reich itself, is concerned not only with the popularization of science, but with the invention of methods directed to cultural ends" (*Universities: American English German,* Second Edition, Oxford University Press, New York, 1931 p. 340).

and England the development has been unmistakably in this direction. Classes may begin with the study of economic problems but before the learning process has gone far the vague consciousness that man does not live by bread alone becomes manifest; the demand that learning shall point the way toward what is euphemistically called the "higher life" is never wholly submerged even among those over-serious persons who wish to improve the world without being conscious of the need of improvement in themselves. The relevancy of the above introductory paragraph and the present chapter is drawn from this presumed and insistent claim that education shall somehow lift us above monotonous necessities into the realm of pure enjoyments.

"Education is preparation for life." How grim and serious and final this sounds! At commencement time life with all its weighty problems is made to fall suddenly upon the shoulders of the educated young. At last they are equipped to face the hard and stubborn world with a will to subdue it, to bring it to terms, to make it yield success. Along the way, contact has been made with a few so-called humanistic or cultural ideas but these after all were offered as decorative badges to be worn as tokens of a "finished" education. Who, indeed, can presume to call himself educated until he can make the same stereotyped references to the classics which his professor has prescribed? Yes, we must have some "culture" to round out the learning process; it may come in packets neatly bound, easily digested, selected from the best academic stocks, and guaranteed not to interfere with the serious business of life, but we must at all costs pay our respects to the goddess of classicism. The question of enjoyment does not enter the equation of this officialized culture—the problem is to get every one inoculated whether he likes it or not. Courageously reversing this process, the leadership of adult education will be able to bring forth new cultural values: instead of indoctrinating students with a preconceived standard of what constitutes good music, painting, literature et cetera, it will begin by discovering what individuals genuinely enjoy. And, if reëducated adults happen to enjoy something which the academicians frown upon, there will be no apologies. Adult education might by such candid means give American art a new impetus; it could at any rate aid greatly in the much-needed procedure of transforming a growing artistic snobbery into an indigenous folk-expression. We can never attain artistic eminence so long as our artists are obliged to secure their training, their inspiration and their standards of appreciation in Europe. On the other hand, our artists can never find a congenial and stimulating environment for their work in this country so long as appreciation remains the inherited prerogative of a coterie of so-called cultured people. In short, adult education may justly be expected to do something toward democratizing art.

At first glance it appears, especially to those who are executively-minded, that "the ideal aim of intelligence seems to be the rational control of human life." [18] But

adults who realize their educational deficiencies are apt
to become too earnest in their search for rationality.
In their determination to run down the reasons for
things they are too frequently tempted to abandon the
joy of things. After all, we ought not to exalt reason
unduly: it was undoubtedly the last of our faculties to
arrive in the fitful march of evolution, and our feelings
are probably still as fundamental as our thoughts. Feelings, sentiments and emotions lie very close to the center
of organic function and are regulative in a degree which
makes thinking seem to be still an uncertain experiment.
But it is useless to discuss feelings and emotions as if
these were aspects of personality separable from thinking
and reasoning. In the present state of our development
these are already interdependent functions and it seems
highly probable that evolution is now proceeding, not
by creating new organs, but by further integrations of
existing organs and functions. It is therefore to be expected that as personalities, that is, partially integrated
unities, we shall need to anticipate our greatest enjoyments, not as pure emotion, but as emotion interpene-
trated with intelligence. Conversely, if adult education
is to save itself from degenerating into another type of
intellectualism, it will teach people how to make their
thinking glow with the warmth of honest feeling. When
driven to definitions modern critics invariably end by
giving art to the emotive or affective phase of personality and science and logic to the reflective or rational
—thus hoping to evade the real issue; this obviously

relegates art to the realm of sheer accident. The alternative assumption seems to be, at least from the viewpoint
of education, that emotions and intelligence are continuous and varying aspects of a single process and that
the finest emotions are those which shine through intelligence, and the finest intelligence that which is reflected
in the light of its appropriate feeling. "I prefer to feel
rather than understand," writes Anatole France in that
exquisite letter to M. Charles Maurice, and then proceeds
to elaborate his understanding. But we cannot feel and
then understand; feelings may predominate over intelligence but they cannot annihilate it; likewise, to understand anything always partakes somewhat of "getting the
feel" of its properties and qualities. Feeling adds warmth
to understanding and understanding gives meaning to
feelings.

Adult educators may well take as their guide in the
realm of appreciation the words of Whitehead: "What
we want is to draw out habits of æsthetic apprehension....
The habit of art is the habit of enjoying vivid values." [19]
"How to bring this sense of order and beauty into the
lives of the ordinary men and women of our country" [20]
constitutes one of the central tasks of adult education.
But we must learn to draw out as well as "bring in"
the sense of beauty since the latter process inevitably runs
the risk of reducing appreciation to passive rather than
creative enjoyment. We get more intense feeling of
beauty and more valid meanings when the "sense of
beauty" is an accompaniment of some activity. Games,

dancing, and the drama may, when not professionalized, furnish the best opportunities for bringing forth values which are susceptible of vivid enjoyment. The highest æsthetic values are probably not those which somehow get themselves registered in books, painting, statues, but rather those which are realized in motion, in participating activity.

Teachers of adult classes who are called to serve in the interest of evoking æsthetic appreciations will be sorely tempted to increase "that already large amount of ineffectual striving for æsthetic conformity" which restrains art from fulfilling its true mission in life. "What then is the function of the serious critics of art and letters, and how do they differ from the tub-thumper, be he more or less refined? Their function is, I imagine, to coöperate with other teaching powers in the development of active intelligence. It is to analyze, explain and illustrate, so that choice may be made relevant to need." [21] And, one might add, so that choice may be made relevant to growth and capacity. No one knows his æsthetic needs until he is well along the road of æsthetic experience. Appreciation is not merely a way of *finding* values; it is also a way of discovering, creating values. Art is essentially a form of mental release; its inception may lie in feelings but its result to the personality is "intellectual enrichment." Artistic experience is immediately enjoyed but also leaves its residue of "enjoyed meanings," to use Dewey's term.[22] And a meaning is always a fermentation which, because of its potential relatedness to other meanings opens the way toward successive enjoyments and enlarged meanings. Their eyes closed to the uses of beauty in life by their preoccupation with the problem of the nature of beauty, tired critics frequently leave the impression that art is an ingenious futility. "Entire freedom from enthusiasm was looked upon as almost equivalent to culture and ripe scholarship," writes Brandes of the second empire,[23] and one surmises that this "second empire" of pedantry becomes the ultimate haven of many professional critics. But appreciation lacks enjoyable content and becomes a new kind of unwarranted specialism—a specialism in unrelated sophistication —whenever critical attitudes eliminate spontaneity and eagerness. Adult education can at least aid in delivering us from that abject fear of expressing our quick and enthusiastic enjoyments—the fear to which we have become habituated under the discipline of professional criticism. There are people who do not know whether they think the play which they have seen is "good" or "bad" until their favorite critic has delivered himself of his oracular judgment in the press the following day. To them, nothing can ever be spontaneously enjoyable— save in a post-mortem conversational sense.

Among intelligent adults an "art-spirit" which can come only through candid and cultivated appreciation is needed. Such a spirit at work among people would inevitably find expression in collective ideals and aspirations. Goldenweiser,[24] speaking of the offices of art in primitive societies, explains in part how art became integrated with life: "The attractiveness and suggestiveness of these symbols, their simultaneous presentation to a large number of devotees, the ease with which multifarious associations are absorbed by these objects, only to be reawakened and refreshed in the minds of the beholder, transform the symbolic art object into a veritable perpetuator of a large part of the culture of a tribe, that part of the culture, moreover, which is emotionally most valuable as well as most clearly representative of the collective ideas of the group." Here we see clearly what is meant by an art-spirit or art-impulse at work in a society. But this is an account of how art became a carrier and intensifier of culture before division of labor sent modern civilizations along new paths of development; the spontaneous flow of art-impulses, which apparently animated pre-civilization societies, has now to make its way as a competitor among many powerful alternatives.

Adult education, it is to be hoped, will revivify this spirit and thereby extend and give new meanings to the values inherent in appreciation. Certainly, art can never be a liberating force in a society which automatically restricts its cultivation to those who have leisure by virtue of their private wealth. Art, its appreciation and enjoyment, belongs to those who have or are capable of having, "intrinsic sensibility" and the highest function of adult education may well be the discovery and release of these qualities of sensibility among the many.

VIII

TO AN AGE OF SPECIALISM

"Effective knowledge is professionalized knowledge, supported by a restricted acquaintance with useful subjects subservient to it. . . .

"This situation has its dangers. It produces minds in a groove. Each profession makes progress, but it is progress in its own groove. . . .

"The dangers arising from this aspect of professionalism are great, particularly in our democratic societies. The directive force of reason is weakened. The leading intellects lack balance. They see this set of circumstances, or that set: but not both sets together. The task of coördination is left to those who lack either the force or the character to succeed in some definite career. In short, the specialized functions of the community are performed better and more progressively, but the generalized direction lacks vision. . . .

"The point is that the discoveries of the nineteenth century were in the direction of professionalism, so that we are left with no expansion of wisdom and with greater need of it. . . . Wisdom is the fruit of balanced development."

—A. N. WHITEHEAD.

"I take it that what the particularist mainly needs is a philosophy and general culture which shall enable him to see his own point of view in something like its true relation to the whole of thought. It is hard to believe, for example, that an economist who also reads Plato or Emerson comprehendingly could adhere to economic determinism."

—CHARLES HORTON COOLEY.

TO AN AGE OF SPECIALISM

THE evils of specialism have been duly noted by college presidents, publicists and philosophers—noticed, verbally proscribed and then left to multiply. Here stands a real dilemma: the division of knowledge goes speedily on with infinity as its goal whereas man's comprehending capacity is distinctly limited. Moreover, knowledge can be expanded only by the method of specialism: when one science or branch of science becomes too complex for complete comprehension by a single mind, its problems must be sub-divided, delimited; succeeding scientists concentrate upon a fraction of the total subject-matter and attain success by means of this very concentration upon particularized objects and processes. Generalization may set new problems but specialism alone discovers new facts.

The moment curricula became responsive to research as distinguished from scholasticism, colleges and universities became subject to the rule of specialization. College presidents who entered the field of education when science was still the intruder and not the controller may remonstrate against specialism as vociferously as they please; faculties will subdivide under their noses. They may go on visualizing the Renaissance ideal of cultured professionalism, but their graduates will continue to be circumscribed specialists who know a great deal about

[75]

one sphere of knowledge and not much about anything else. Indeed, the phenomenal quantitative expansion of colleges and universities during the past two decades may be regarded, in part at least, as a direct response to specialization. Higher education, so-called, has come to be predominantly a form of vocational training.

Industry presents the same picture. Reformists may bemoan the fact that the modern factory-worker sees merely a small portion of the finished product and does not understand its relationship to the whole. Ten years hence he will see even a smaller portion. Mass production can succeed only by eliminating so far as possible all waste motion—an act which can apparently be achieved only by subdividing and simplifying the individual worker's task. The man who now places a nut on a bolt and gives six turns in passing may later give three turns, and eventually one. Indeed, he may come at last to be merely a tender of machines which perform all other necessary manipulative functions.

Development of less than a century of applied science has thrown government into veritable chaos. The older concept of the political state is no longer tenable. The significant problems which confront modern states are primarily technical, not political, in character. The British Parliament is asked to decide a crucial question concerning coal mines: Can the mines be managed under private ownership and at the same time pay wages sufficient for a decent standard of life, and if so, how? Here is a question which involves technological information with respect to mining efficiency; economic information as to foreign markets, distribution, capitalization, et cetera; and sociological factors relevant to a decent standard of living. But this is precisely the sort of a question with which a democratically-chosen parliament is least able to deal. In fact, the problem involved is given political reference, not because it is political in character but because its consequences disturb the order and unity of the state. In a moment of crisis the government of the United States began construction of a gigantic hydro-electric plant in one of the southern states. Congress has ever since been debating the question of its disposal: cast in the political mold, the problem became, not what is the efficient course of action, but how can this technical question be decided in terms of party prestige and sectional advantage, that is, how can a technical matter be made to appear political.

Suggested escapes from the dilemma of specialism may be condensed into three general propositions:

I. In academic *education* experiments proceed in three directions: [25]

1. Required *orientation or survey courses* which are designed to give the student a broad and comprehensive acquaintance with world history, the evolution of civilization, the growth of ideas, the span of social and political progress, the march of science, the requirements of citizenship, et cetera.

2. Curriculum adjustments which provide for a limited amount of specialization within a context of broad fundamental training.

3. Restriction of undergraduate study to so-called liberal subjects and reserving intensive specialization for post-graduates.

Criticisms (a) Orientation courses are likely to contribute to superficial knowledge of many facts without understanding of their depth and significance. Such courses are chiefly useful in aiding students to discover interests and dispositions. (b) Limited specialization does not meet the demands of the present generation of college students; they want technical and "practical" courses which can be put to use. (c) Graduate study is still considered—perhaps deservedly—to be a luxury suitable possibly for the person doomed to a life of scholarship but not worthy of the man of action. The weight of the above criticism falls directly upon educational misconceptions, and chiefly upon that misconception which regards education as a reflex of industry. So long as our primary standards of valuation are pecuniary, educational institutions will be able to make but feeble resistances to specialism.

II. In *industry* escape is for the most part sought in:

1. Trade Unionism, or collective struggles for increased wages, decreased hours of labor and improved conditions.

2. Works' councils or various schemes for coördinating the various specialized elements in the industry.

3. A wider participation in recreations and amusements after working hours.

4. Psychic compensation in the form of allegiance to some Utopian scheme for reorganizing the whole of economic life and thereafter the incentives and satisfactions of life itself.

Criticism: (a) Trade Unionism, insofar as it does not get itself translated into new practices within industry, remains a fighting and not a creating, educating force; so long as its aims are merely to get more or less of what its members already have, it will be a compensation for specialized labor, not a solution for its inherent problems. (b) This criticism holds true for the remaining three avenues of escape; each of these methods leaves the individual worker still a specialist whose daily tasks call forth diminishing fractions of his personality. (Industrial managers, technicians, bosses—those whose work gives them a sense of being in control—are caught in the same trap; they are perhaps less conscious of the disservices of specialism because of a wider range of sociable and recreational opportunities in the community.)

III. In *government*,[26] among the numerous proposals to be considered, the most significant are:

1. Commissions, boards and other extra-or quasi- or semi-governmental bodies composed of experts and frequently endowed with judicial and executive powers but usually restricted to advisory recommendations made either to the executive, judicial or legislative branches of government (Interstate Commerce Commission, Tariff Commission, e.g.).

2. Employment of municipal managers, technologists with engineering training, who are vested with powers of decision over technical issues—sometimes sharing this authority with a small body of elected commissioners or aldermen.

3. Wider use of technical experts by governmental departments.

4. Restricting the decision of popular suffrage to the selection of persons and not to choice between issues.

Criticism: As will be noted at once all of these schemes tend to increase specialization while they leave the citizen with diminished functions. He, the citizen, is not to grow into fuller citizenship by these means; on the contrary, to be a citizen under the rule of experts is to be restricted to giving a mild "yes" or an emphatic "no" to some one else's decisions. But this reduces citizenship to a false logical base; questions which can be answered by yes or no are seldom worth asking. When the function of citizenship loses its creativeness it also loses its meaning.

We are committed, it must be repeated, to the process of division of labor, to specialism. The problem resolves itself ultimately into the query: *How can society secure the highest services of specialists?* We may get a very efficient service of experts in one of two ways: by subordinating them to the will of a dictator who determines the ends for which they shall labor, or by transferring executive powers to specialists themselves. In either case, we must be prepared to make corresponding sacrifices. Admittedly, more efficient results will be accomplished when power tends to become absolute and centralized. But is this the highest service we may expect of specialists? Power vested in dictators and executive specialists means power taken from the citizen. It may be that citizens make poor use of power when they possess it, but that consideration is for the moment irrelevant. When the sense of power is gone, what incentives are left for the increase of knowledge? The functions of citizenship, like all functions, atrophy when not used.

Our choice is not limited to leaving the experts alone, subordinating them to dictators, or placing them under the control of poorly informed publics. But one hesitates to propose alternatives. The signs are none too hopeful. It may be that democracy reared on impossible metaphysical foundations must decay more or less completely

before we find our way with science. Mussolini may be
the true prophet of our time.* Liberalism, democracy
and parliamentary government may, as he so vehemently
affirms, have fulfilled their functions. At any rate, the
liberal has lost his effectiveness, parliaments have ceased
to function, or function badly, and democracy is fast
becoming a term used to denote illusion. Yet, I do not
regard these as signals of despair; the fact that our
modern political, economic and social structures and
processes are disintegrating makes experiment feasible.
We have once more reached one of those historical

---

* EDITOR'S NOTE: What Linderman, writing in 1927, a
year after the publication of "Adult Education" really thought
about Mussolini and Fascism is clarified by the following statement: "Fascism and bolshevism are two social forces with which
the twentieth century must somehow come to terms. Bolshevism,
we are beginning to learn after ten years of apprehension and
phobia, has little or no significance for the United States; we
are a bourgeois nation. What occurs in the republic of soviets
will continue to interest us as world citizens because it may
also happen elsewhere; but what is taking place in the Italian
peninsula should interest us as Americans because it may some
day happen here.

Mussolini obviously was not joking when he told a representative of the Associated Press some months ago that he
found more parallels for fascism in the United States than
anywhere else in the world. Our men of affairs discover that
they can swim easily and comfortably in the waters of fascism
—over there.

Just because fascism could so easily be made compatible
with large sectors of American thought and practice it constitutes
the first realistic challenge to the spirit of freedom and democracy which emerged from our revolution in 1776" (From
Robert Gessner, Editor, *The Democratic Man: Selected Writings
of Eduard C. Lindeman,* Beacon Press, Boston, 1956, p. 239).

periods which seems like a dead-end because the shell of old institutions and habits, although crumbling, still possesses sufficient resiliency to prevent the new from bursting forth. In like periods of the past, thinkers with vision turned occasion to account by imagining and portraying perfect societies, Utopias. The function of Utopias is to set activity toward new goals, to visualize the consequences of changed conduct, to re-direct ideals. We need not lose ourselves in fanciful, legendary and unrealizable dreams but if we do not utilize our present difficulties as opportunities for equally adventurous challenges to the future, we shall deserve to be recorded a generation of people who possessed many things but lacked courage and vision for high ventures.

Possibilities for promising experiments lie open in many directions but we must confine our discussion to those which seem especially pertinent to our present theme. In the first place, experts and specialists whose functions become external to the people whom they serve have been miseducated. They have, in Cooley's [27] words, become "particularists," that is, persons who behave as if "one phase of the process" were "the source of all others." Consequently the impact of their function, when it includes educative contact (which is seldom), is forever education in a false direction. The specialist who becomes protagonist for a particularist point of view has already deserted the spirit of science; he labors under the *"illusion of centrality"* which keeps him and his disciples from recognizing "that the life-process is an evolving whole of mutually interacting parts, any of which is effect as well as cause." Specialists can contribute to the increase of wisdom (as distinguished from knowledge) by dealing with parts in such manner that they become useful in explaining wholes. Educational institutions can, of course, assist in this program by acknowledging that one of the primary aims of learning is to induce an "organic view" of life; they can discover how it happens that students develop blind-spots—those negative adaptations which pave the way for specialism. But in the end specialists and experts must conduct experiments in the atmosphere of their functions. It is one thing to hold an intellectual conviction against particularism and quite another to live organically—especially if living means making one's way in competition with other specialists. We shall secure the highest services of experts when they learn to integrate their functions with respect to specific problems. Integration is not a verbal exercise but a method by which active differences interpenetrate. Six medical specialists, each examining that portion of the organism upon which he has specialized, will come away with six varying explanations of cause and effect; their specialized knowledge can be fruitfully integrated only when the six points of view are focussed upon the organism as a whole.

Specialists can, then, help to save themselves and us as well by integrating their functions. But this is not enough. We, the objects of specialists' attention, must somehow become aware of what is being done to us and

with us; we must become active particpants in the pro-
ess. At this point many thinkers abandon the trail; over-
whelmed by the complexity of modern knowledge and the
paucity of intelligence, they fall back upon some externalism, some easy division: government of the lesser minds
by the best, master and servant, commanders and obeyers,
executives and submissives, knowers and doers, et cetera.
The problem, however, will not be dismissed so readily:
when our division seems fixed and secure in one sphere,
flux breaks out in another. The only relatively permanent
method for "keeping people in their places" is to vest
power in hereditary castes. Even then biological processes
tend to defeat our purposes. But there is another and
simpler approach. We capitulate to experts because we
attempt to understand too much, and failing in this, we
abandon the ways of intelligence altogether. My conception of adult education points toward a continuing process
of evaluating experiences, a method of awareness through
which we learn to become alert in the discovery of meanings. Now the specialist enters the equation of our lives
when meanings have become confused or lost; we stand
baffled in the face of an adjustment lacking courage for
the next step because we have no sure knowledge of what
it may mean to us. The expert cuts the cord of uncer-
tainty; he speaks as one having authority, and we, having
transferred decision to him, act upon his word and thereby
achieve the adjdustment. But alas, this is merely a superficial aspect of the true adjusting process. When next we
confront a similar difficulty, another expert will need

to be consulted; in the end, if this were the essence of expert service, life would become a chronic succession of consultations in the presence of specialists. The only meanings possible would be those purchasable from experts. This is, however, precisely what any person with a grain of intellectual self-respect will refuse to do—to take his meanings second-hand. An adjustment precipitates meanings when it facilitates future adjustments, that is, when it is accompanied by an intellectual process which becomes instrumental to the whole of intelligence. We consult, for example, an oculist because we have been annoyed by difficulties in reading. (The sequence of adjustment: annoyance felt, difficulty recognized, cause of difficulty discovered, cause removed, difficulty lessened, annoyance diminished.) We begin by contributing to his technique since he could not diagnose the difficulty properly without knowing what effects it had produced. Insofar as our interpretation corresponds with his external observation, we are both engaged in discovery. Now, the ordinary layman cannot be expected to know all the intricacies of eye-structure and function but here is one isolated feature which is of primary interest to him at the moment. How much of this can he comprehend? If he can understand merely enough to be intelligent in carrying out the oculist's instructions, the experience will have been profitable. If he can understand sufficient to experiment with his reading-habits, to see some of the relations between cause and effect and to seek improvement within this relation, he will have participated in a true educative experience. And if he can see further into the relations between the use of his eyes and his total bodily functions, he will begin to experience meanings—that is, be in a position to gather the fruits of real learning. We can utilize expert functions for educative purposes if we begin by giving attention to those relevant features which are within our capacities. When we comprehend relevant portions, i.e., relevant to our present interest, of what the expert is doing, we are in position to become participants in the expert's services.

In conclusion, opportunities for turning experience to account educationally will be multiplied if we delimit the area of our functions as well as the size of our problems. Experience, the stuff out of which education is grown, is after all a homely matter. The affairs of home, neighborhood and local community are vastly more important educationally than those more distant events which seem so enchanting. Experience is, first of all, doing something; second, doing something that makes a difference; third, knowing what difference it makes. Our personalities count for something; we enjoy experiences in proportion to the effectiveness of our actions. Now it is all very wholesome to join with world societies dedicated to bring peace to mankind, but peace will come only when individual human beings learn to act, to behave in the direction of peace. Blessed is the man whose talk bears a direct relation to his acts. Otherwise, behavior and conversation may become so far separated as to dissociate aspects of personality. We can always talk glibly about problems, yes, even suggest the only possible solution, when we are far enough removed from the scene to allow our activities to escape the consequences of our talk. We can all be experts—a long way from home. And somehow modern life tends to accelerate our long-distance propensities. Each new invention in the field of communication is at first greeted as another boon to human relations. Does it not bring us closer together? And will we not therefore learn to have more respect for and good-will toward each other? This naïve manner of placing human relations upon the quantity-contact basis probably stands in the way of our making the best use of communication inventions. It undoubtedly causes us to overlook the fact that highly-developed means of communication are indispensable to highly-centralized forms of social control. Some important differences persisted in the various regions of the United States before we all read the same syndicated news, listened to the same radio announcers, witnessed the same motion pictures, ate the same food, wore the same clothes, et cetera. Rapid means of transportation and communication tend to standardize us and therefore render us easier of control by single authorities.

The life of simplicity is gone forever. Telephones, radios, aeroplanes, automobiles as well as specialists are integral to our industrialized civilization and we must work our way through, not around, them. The present argument allows for as many conveniences and as many experts as we can afford—and as many as we can understand. Our personalities can be redeemed if we insist upon a proper share in the solution of problems which specifically concern us. This means giving more attention to small groups; it means as much decentralization, diversity and local autonomy as is consistent with order. Indeed, we may well sacrifice order, if enforced externally, for valid difference. Our hopes flow from the simple conviction that diversity is more likely to make life interesting than is conformity, and from the further conviction that active participation in interesting affairs furnishes proper stimulations for intellectual growth. The chief disservice for which specialism is accountable is externalism; specialists ask too little of us. And they will ask still less in the future unless we supply enough intelligence to bridge the gap between experts and experience.

IX

AS DYNAMIC FOR COLLECTIVE
ENTERPRISE

"The problem is not how to produce great men, but how to produce great societies."

—A. N. WHITEHEAD.

"Modern life is complicated by the fact that we pursue our most vital interests not as individuals but as members of organized groups. Questions of conduct, therefore, are apt to take the form not simply of what is right or wrong for one of us to do, but of what is best to do under circumstances that require co-operation with others of our group or of other groups who may not shares our views. Our social ideals, therefore—such ideals as godliness, patriotism, liberty, charity, democracy—must get something more than a vague mass acceptance. In the organized society of to-day our movements are complex. The 'plot' of its collective life is dramatic: its action centers on the revaluating of these ideals—on applying them to situations within which must be encompassed an adjustment of various interests. To play their due part these interests must first be understood, and to be understood they must be allowed to speak for themselves."

—A. D. SHEFFIELD.

AS DYNAMIC FOR COLLECTIVE
ENTERPRISE

EMPHASIS has been placed in the foregoing chapters upon education with respect to individual personalities. Education has been viewed as a process which goes on within psycho-physical organisms—organisms whose objectives range from satisfaction of simple physiological needs to intellectual curiosity concerning the universe itself. Education is behaving and behavior is a manifestation of activity of a discreet organism. Again, education is peculiarly a kind of behavior through which organisms attempt to adjust themselves to external or internal factors which, having set up frictions, call for new adjustment. Without the compulsions of struggle, learning could never have arisen as a means of adjustment. Friction, strain, struggle, conflict, tension, stress: these are states or situations which cannot endure since they are always accompanied by pain; consequently organisms strive by every means within their capacity to find an adjustment which will free them from painful feelings. Most of the energy generated or made potential by the metabolic process, save that utilized in habitual, automatized behavior, is consumed by these adjusting and readjusting activities.

If, then, we want to know what education is good for, we must ask: What kinds of adjustments are being required of individuals? After we have determined the nature of impending adjustments we then need to inquire: In what ways can education aid and accelerate the adjusting process? Further refined, our question becomes: What kinds of learning will lead toward adjustments which in turn lead to higher adjustments? Or, is our scheme of education compatible with an evolutionary concept of growing personalities?

We have already seen that evolving personalities follow the path of learning in an attempt to adjust themselves to a world in which knowledge leads to power, power leads to self-expression, freedom and creativity, creative freedom leads to enjoyable experience, and finally, a world in which knowledge goes forward under a discipline of specialization. These considerations as stated converge to emphasize individual aspects of education. We now must recognize the fact that these qualities which are enhanced by intellectual effort become meaningful only when seen in social contexts. Intelligence, like freedom, is relative, not merely to ignorance or to bondage, but also to intelligence and freedom in other human beings. Education proceeds by means of communication, and all forms of communication are social products. Self-expression takes on meaning in relation to other selves. Behavior belongs to individuals but conduct is social.

From many sources of social theory and social practice comes the insistent appeal to bring people together, to overcome individualism. The call is gratuitous. People are

being brought together, willy-nilly. They have no alternative. Every persistent need of the human organism is
brought soon or late within the area of collective means.
Vital needs left without the scope of collectivity, either
as control or means, eventuate as incidences of unadjust-
ment. The individualist of modern life not only finds his
normal aspirations baulked but he himself becomes an
inhibition to the enhancement of his own aims.

The potential needs of the human organism are un-
limited. Each need satisfied releases energies which flow
into channels of renewed discontent; the new or unused
energy disrupts the harmony of life, or is dissipated.
And, most needs lie without the organism,—are environmental. To meet the need is to confront the environment
—the socialized environment of the modern world. Man
does not "make up his mind" to be social. He is caught
within a social *milieu.* He is social by virtue of his enlarg-
ing needs. He cannot even select the precise kind of
sociality within whose circle he must function to meet
these needs.

Obnoxious as the view may be to all who cling to
intellectual predispositions of individualism this is the
realism with which modern man must come to terms.
The tenderminded patriot proclaims: There are no
classes! His orotund eloquence is soon modulated to con-
form to the atmosphere of the committee-room, where,
if he succeeds in initiating activity, he must deal with
classes. The farmer may not wish to belong to a class,

but his collective activities are exempted by statues from certain restraints imposed upon the collective activities of business corporations. Coal miners may not belong to a class but when the conglomerate of classes wants coal, the patriot must deal with representatives of collectivist coal miners. No logical squirmings or sentimental predilections can overcome the reality of so much realism. Nor can the problem be approached by subtle intellectual maneuvers. Some people who cannot honestly evade the recognition of classes in the functional sense, insist that their real objection is not to classes but to class-consciousness. The distinction is not without merit. It splits life into discrete compartments and the particles may be more easily manipulated than the whole. In substance the position of the intellectual individualist is dualistic; he says: Be a member of your class if you must but see to it that your mind does not find you out. Act collectively but think individualistically. Join the trade union but do not become a trade unionist. Collectivism in function —individualism in thought!

Modern psychology may be considerably confused about many things but on this point it is both logically and empirically clear: "Beware how you isolate thinking from doing." The potential revolutions of the future are incipient in the current hiatus between thought and activity. Thinking as a process of rationalizing—how this good word has suffered!—activity in terms of reality must assume contemporaneous qualities. Activity in the present with corresponding thought-evaluation in the past represents man's persistent dilemma. When thinking is unable to catch up with doing, the results of the doing eventuate in man's undoing. In a primary sense, modern collectivism has its roots in science and industrial technique whereas individualism has its origins in historical, philosophical and religious traditions. The application of science to materials in the effort to meet evolving human needs leads inevitably to cumulative collectivism. The material compulsion *ris a tergo* is to live the collective life. On the psychological side stands the equal compulsion to think the collective life. Bankers, manufacturers, merchants, wage-earners, physicians, teachers, farmers— all must pool their interests under definite forms of collective action or suffer the defeat of those interests. Collectivism is the road to power, the predominant reality of modern life. To exercise that power without integration with the intellectual process is to court social suicide. Collectivism in function with a corresponding individualism in thought produces a divided social structure, an uncontrollable social organization and a mystifying social process.

How can education supply directive energy for collective enterprises? The most concise answer is threefold: (a) by revealing the nature of the social process; (b) by transforming the battle of interests from warfare into creative conflict; (c) by developing a method for social functions which will make the collective life an educational experience. The first two points will be briefly considered here and the last forms the theme for our concluding chapter.

The social process is essentially a "contact between minds".[28] The *"community* of me and you" represents the beginning of society. Minds which interact remain forever functions of separate organisms; the relations *between* constitute social phenomena. There is no super-mind, no group-mind, which is a summation of individual minds, but there are, as Burns aptly states, "mind-groups," that is, psychological resultants of the relation between separate minds. Let us imagine four persons, A, B, C and D, responding to each other with A as the innovator or initiator of contact. B then responds to A with the result that B's response is b x a; C now responds to (b x a) or BA and his total response is c x (b x a); D's response is d x [c x (x a)], et cetera. We see that each succeeding response carries with it not merely additions of previous response and stimuli but rather inter-penetrated relations between (indicated by the multiplication sign x) foregoing relations. This process goes on in all sorts of contact between persons and it at once becomes apparent that the resulting relations will evolve as meanings or understandings in proportion to the degree in which each responding person is intelligent about the quality of his response and its direction. Many frictions on the level of social relations arise from the fact that we respond to others dishonestly or unintelligently. Once we become aware of the fact that our responses emerge as new relations which in turn become stimuli directing and influencing all future responses, we begin to see how important it is to make our contacts with others an intellectual concern.

Next we need to understand how it happens that we get involved in groups, associations, collectivities which formulate standards of behavior. We sooner or later come to feel that we cannot always follow our desires and wishes; we need to ask how our proposed act will be evaluated by some group or groups to which we have given allegiance. An individual trade unionist may not wish to go on strike but if his union has through its officials called a strike, he will follow their orders, not his wishes. A citizen may regard his nation's war as an iniquity but when the government has opened hostilities he too will be conscripted. Situations of this sort are usually confronted with ethical principles: what is the right or the wrong course of action? Pacifists will, for example, decide the problem of war in advance and on purely ethical grounds. The basic moral principle of the pacifist—inviolability of the individual conscience— assumes that in a conflict between individual and group the higher values lie with the individual. This procedure, of course, prejudges the specific issue: the pacifist, like all absolutists, comes into situations, not with an open-minded desire for facts, but with determination that however the problem is solved his *a priori* solution is to undergo no alteration. Consequently, few educational influences emerge from pacifist propaganda; situations which can be met by the simple process of applying a preconceived general rule need not be dealt with intelligently.* In addition, these general rules which force conduct into channels already marked out prevent even moralists from exercising a truly moral influence; evolving, creative, intelligent conduct flies out of the window when absolutism enters the door. Infallibility and wisdom hold nothing in common.

Ethics of the either-or variety falsify situations involving conflicts between individuals and groups. Objectivity is lost the moment individual conduct is conceived as something separable from social conduct. Values arise

----

* EDITOR'S NOTE: At the end of World War II and subsequently, Lindeman, in his writings and speeches, displayed concern over "peacetime conscription", rejected "military preparation as a reasonable method for ending war", and referred to the tendency for the threat of "imminent" war to "destroy all other human values". See Robert Gessner, Editor, *The Democratic Man,* pp. 290, 209-302, and 343-344. Compare his early version of pacifism, as a form of absolutism, with that of Albert Einstein, whom Lindeman regarded as the ideal type of scientist-citizen. In Einstein's view "He who cherishes the values of culture cannot fail to be a pacifist" (Otto Nathan and Heinz Norden, *Einstein On Peace,* Simon and Schuster, New York — Musson Books, Toronto — 1961, pp. 54 and 55). But, ". . . in the early years of Nazism in Germany, he (Einstein) announced that he was no longer able to advocate the policy of war resistance which he had so passionately promoted in the preceding years. He then came under particularly severe attack by the pacifist movement, but he himself never felt he had forsaken the cause of pacifism, and continued to consider himself a convinced and devoted pacifist, one who was unable to adhere to a rigid policy in the face of changing circumstances" (Ibid., p. x, from the "Introduction" by Otto Nathan).

out of the social process; what is called "conscience" is merely a system of beliefs or fears which epitomize socially derived valuations. If we turn our attention to the functional groupings which characterize modern life, we begin to realize that social organizations are means for achieving individual ends. We merge our personalities with other personalities because we believe that our interests will thereby be advanced. Society is a process, not an end or goal—a process of interacting individuals. Collectivism is a representation of individual interests.[29] Groups will arise whenever two or more people identify a common interest which to them seems worthy of perpetuation or enhancement. And, conflicts between groups will occur so long as interests are variable. Education for collective life begins when interests are intelligently scrutinized and validified, and since interests vary continuously in growing personalities, this validifying process must continue so long as we regard ourselves as functional beings. Modern life calls for increasing varieties of adjustment to collective techniques; if education cannot direct collective enterprises into creative channels, we are doomed to a warfare between groups in which unrelated power and ruthlessness remain the only criteria of survival.

"We are born to struggle as the sparks fly upward, but not necessarily to brutality and waste." And, we are destined to prosecute our interests collectively, but not necessarily by defeating or annihilating other groups. Nor can we find our way in placid acquiescence, in sacrifice of our interests. To overcome and to be over-come are both negative procedures. Sentimentality is often more mischievous than savagery.

We need to be candid concerning our interests and candor implies willingness to submit our claims to every conceivable test. Employers who offer wages less than they expect to pay, trade unionists who ask for more than they expect to get, politicians who represent private interests under the guise of public service—these are falsifications of the social process. How absurd to pretend that we can get what we want by concealing what we want! And, how tragic to reduce social relations to the barren status of unscrupulous bargaining. Our alternative is "open diplomacy"—the assumption that what we want is worth wanting, possesses sufficient integrity to stand comparison and is capable of making its way on merits and not through coercion.

But honesty is not enough; it is easily conceivable that conflict among honest people might result in nothing more than unintegrated righteousness. Religionists are often enough honest in their convictions but the conflict implies that factors which are now in opposition are capable of synthesis. Diversity is eternal but specific diversities rise to creative levels when they combine to produce new unities. We need to learn, not merely to be frank, but to make frankness articulate. Intelligent, ex-plicit, unconfused presentation of difference provides a setting for our interests from which valid meanings may be expected.[30] These are requisites for creative conflict.

We are now on the threshold, equipped with proper attitudes and dispositions but still incapable of transforming collective warfare into creative conflict. Method is still lacking. Like the scientist, we may foresee what research and experiment may bring forth but until we have developed a method for taking the next step, our foreknowledge remains impotent. The vast unused stores of energy which are potential in collective enterprises will be released when we become intelligent enough to discover ways of turning wasteful warfare into productive integrations. For, after all, conflict is not in itself creative. It is merely preliminary to experiments which may or may not emerge as creative resultants.

Social organization has long been a favorite subject for speculation and generalization; the present demand is for specific analysis. We know almost nothing concerning the multiform changes in conduct which flow from responses to collective enterprises, and the various aspects of group functioning, such as representation, consent, leadership, et cetera, are still shrouded in mystery or submerged in traditions. And this is peculiarly the sphere in which conscious experimentation is most likely to prove fruitful. Man can affect his biological future slightly; he can develop but probably not increase his intellectual capacity; these being avenues of evolution which have apparently achieved completion or near-completion. And even the meager opportunities for biological and mental improvement are dependent upon the discovery and utilization of social means.

Adult education as a movement is here presented with a challenging opportunity. Adults who go forth on the long road which leads to intelligence will discover before they have traveled far that mere self-improvement is a delusion. Intelligence is itself a relative term—a term which possesses little or no meaning save when used as a comparative. One individual is intelligent—less or more —with respect to other persons; and the significant components of his intelligence are derivatives of social processes. So-called native intelligence is not in reality intelligence but merely capacity for accumulating or developing intelligence. Functional intelligence is social in its origins, in its materials and in its uses. Consequently, we do not pursue the path of learning solely for the purpose of putting more knowledge into our own behavior. Knowing-behavior, which is intelligence, is social in two directions: it takes others into account and it calls forth more intelligent responses from others. If then learning adults wish to live in a social environment in which their intellectual alertness will count for something (will get itself realized, i.e., in power, creative expression, freedom, et cetera) they will be as eager to improve their collective enterprises, their groups, as they are to improve themselves. Orthodox education may be a preparation for life but adult education is an agitating instrumentality for changing life. Institutions, groups and organizations come within the scope of continuing, advancing learning insofar as these collective agencies furnish the medium for educational experience. When collective functions no longer make room for the free play of intellectual diversity, they abandon the right to claim allegiance from intelligent persons. It is no accident that the most virile adult education of our time parallels functional organizations: farmer-coöperators of Denmark and trade unionists of Great Britain. Adult education will become an agency of progress if its short-time goal of self-improvement can be made compatible with a long-time, experimental but resolute policy of changing the social order. Changing individuals in continuous adjustment to changing social functions—this is the bilateral though unified purpose of adult learning. Manifestly, these aims cannot be realized until adult educators evolve a method adequate to the purpose.

X

IN TERMS OF METHOD

"A method which permits us to determine only cases of stereotyped activity and leaves us helpless in the face of changed conditions is not a scientific method at all, and becomes less and less practically useful with the continual increase of fluidity in modern social life."

—W. I. THOMAS.

"In the root sense of the words, instruction is building in, whereas education is leading out."

—C. P. CONGER.

IN TERMS OF METHOD

ADULT education is a process through which learners become aware of significant experience. Recognition of significance leads to evaluation. Meanings accompany experience when we know what is happening and what importance the event includes for our personalities. A friend comes excitedly into your presence exclaiming: "I have had an experience!" Immediately you become consciously expectant: you want to know what has caused this new vivification of his personality and what interpretation he will place upon it. If you know him intimately, you will make quick guesses: he usually sees difficulties where others see opportunities and therefore you feel certain that his interpretation will be in the direction of pessimism; or he sees opportunities where others see difficulties and therefore you know that whatever has happened will be incorporated into his personality as an added increment of optimism. In either case you will be observing a personality in the process of evaluating experience; you see him in a new and dramatic setting and you know that whatever meaning he attaches to his experience it will either enrich or impoverish his life.

The real distinction between educated and uneducated persons is not to be found in such superficial criteria as academic degrees, formal study or accumulation of facts; indeed, formal learning may, and often does, lead people into narrow scholarship and out of life. Educated persons find their satisfactions in bringing knowledge to bear upon experience, and the best-informed person is still ignorant if his knowing is not also a lively ingredient of his living. But it is not wholly correct to say, "Bring knowledge to bear upon experience"; knowledge, rather, emerges from experience. Intelligence is the light which reveals educational opportunities in experience. Life is experiencing and intelligent living is a way of making experience an educational adventure. To be educated is not to be informed but to find illumination in informed living. Periods of intellectual awakening are correctly named "enlightenments" for it is then that lovers of wisdom focus the light of learning upon experience and thereby discover new meanings for life, new reasons for living.

Our lives are successive valuations of experience: in youth we need to extract from life its highest yield of emotional experience (how fatal it is when schools attempt to make little intellectuals out of children who need so much to *feel* the world!) but if intelligence does not enter to temper, to give meaning to emotions, we shall grow old without growing up. Growth should be a process of integrating emotions with thought, an evolving capacity for feeling more deeply and thinking more clearly. Educative experience spans the whole of life. And experience proceeds from any situation to which adjustment is made with accompanying mental release. Experiences can never happen twice for we move forward into time as changing organisms; education, by the same token, can never stop without abandoning personality to the barren existence of instinctive, habitual responses. Even cynics who pretend that all experience ends in illusion continue to intellectualize their illusions, to search for the meaning of meaningless life.

Conventional education has somehow become enslaved to a false premise: knowledge is conceived to be a precipitation, a sediment of the experience of others; it is neatly divided into subjects which in turn are parcelled out to students, not because students express eagerness or interest, but because the subjects fit into a traditional scheme —so much mathematics, so much history, so much language, et cetera, and above all so much regard for disciplinary values as to make even the study of interesting subjects an uninteresting task. Happy the student whose teacher knows more than his subject. And brave the teacher who dares to reveal his special subject in the context of the whole of life and learning.

Subjects, we need to be reminded, are merely convenient labels for portions of knowledge to which specialists have given attention. Research is probably clarified by the departmentalizing of knowledge; the investigator who calls himself an economist will undoubtedly profit by delimiting the area of his inquiry, by specifying his problems. If, on the other hand, teachers assume that education can be achieved by the same procedure, they will ultimately succeed in reversing the true educative process; their students will be induced to view education as mastery of subjects instead of mastery of life. After all, it requires no more than common insight to perceive that life does not present itself to us in the form of experiences some of which may be labeled economic, some psychic, some social, some linguistic, et cetera. It may be well enough to be taught that there are phenomena which are predominantly economic, et cetera, but there can never be a purely economic experience. The falsest view of life, as in the fable of the blindfolded men and the elephant, is one which rests upon some particularism as its point of reference. For example, in purchasing a pair of shoes a man certainly goes through motions which fit the category of economics; but no economist who is not also aware of the psychological cogitations which have preceded the sale can make a proper interpretation of the event; and these mental preliminaries are also accompanied by social implications: one does not buy even a pair of shoes without in some manner influencing or being influenced by others. Did the man buy the right pair of shoes—right with respect to the shape of his foot, the kind of use to which the shoes will be put, his income, his knowledge of leather and shoe-manufacturing? Did he pay the right price? Were the shoes made in a union shop? Was the salesman who sold the shoes under-paid? This is, of course, an absurd refinement of illustration but it requires a simple absurdity to demonstrate how pedantic it is to assume that we can understand life by studying subjects.

Many educators who have come to realize that most of their subject-matter disappears from the minds of students shortly after graduation fall back upon the consolation that at least students have been disciplined—they will know how to find knowledge even if they do not possess it. This apology carries the premise another step in the wrong direction: our minds, our personalities, are not repositories into which knowledge is dumped in the hope that it can be reclaimed in the hour of need. If we could fish in the waters of memory for needed knowledge, our catches would be perpetual disappointments: knowledge like fish, either grows or dies. And if knowledge grows, it is because knowing was once a part of experiencing.

Arguments directed against the subject-approach in education, even when sufficiently forceful to win intellectual approval of educators, will make little headway until accompanying experiments are made possible. Our conventional system of education—from kindergarten to university—is committed to subjects. Preoccupation with the content of education has so far overbalanced pedagogical thought that schoolmen now find their center of interest in curriculum-making: the process of transforming the school into a department-store bargain counter. The system derives its chief momentum from subject-teaching—a method which is compatible with a perverted and shallow pragmatism and profitable to an industrial order which requires technicians, not educated men and women. The method is also congenial to, if indeed it did not evolve from, the conception which views education as something from which one graduates. How could the various "points" and entrance requirements and degree requisites be determined—how, indeed, would any one know when education was finished—if institutions of learning were deprived of this convenient measuring-rod of subjects? Happily, students of the universities and colleges possess wit enough to see the serio-comic response which is made to subject-controlled education: they call those who take it all too seriously "credit-baggers" and "degree-hunters."

Adult education, happily, requires neither entrance nor exit examinations. Adult learners attend classes voluntarily and they leave whenever the teaching falls below the standard of interest. What they learn converges upon life, not upon commencement and diploma. The external tokens of education are removed so that the learning process may stand or fall on its intrinsic merits. (It would be an *experience* for conventional teachers who call the roll, cover the subject in so many weeks, and grade their students within a fraction of a point if they had to make their way as teachers on no other basis than ability to interest voluntary students.) And because adult education is free from the yoke of subject-tradition, its builders are able to experiment boldly even in the sacrosanct sphere of pedagogical method. Indeed, if adult education is to produce a difference of quality in the use of intelligence, its promoters will do well to devote their major concern to method and not content.

Life is confronted in the form of situations, occasions which necessitate action. Education is a method for giving situations a setting, for analyzing complex wholes into manageable, understandable parts, and a method which points out the path of action which, if followed, will bring the circumstance within the area of experiment. Since that education is best which most adequately helps us to meet situations, the best teaching method is one which emerges from situation-experiences. Or, in Dewey's words, "The trained mind is one that best grasps the degree of observation, forming of ideas, reasoning and experimental testing required in any special case, and that profits the most, in future thinking, by mistakes made in the past. What is important is that the mind should be sensitive to problems and skilled in methods of attack and solution." [31] We shall have need, before any given situation is properly confronted, of all the relevant experience of others which bears upon our case —experience which has been stored away in books and that which comes freshly from researches and expert knowledge.

Situations arise when our aims or purposes are impeded, when our wishes fall beneath our present capacities. Conscious effort needs therefore to be directed along two channels: (a) inward toward the wish, its incidence, its validity, its realizability and its integrity with respect to our total personality; and (b) outward toward the circumstances which, for the moment, act as barriers to the fulfillment of the wish. This analysis of the situation furnishes the first set of problems with which we shall have to deal. A college professor writes to explain the situation in which he finds himself with respect to an antagonistic administration. He is not, so far as his description reveals, aware of any problem arising within his personality. Before a letter—suggesting that he make an analysis of his situation in terms of his past activities and their contributory relation to his purposes—can reach him, he is discharged and now writes for recommendations for another position. He is over-conscious of the outward circumstances and is therefore not capable of sensitizing himself for the inner analysis. The situation has led to no educative experiences and his present mood of resentment will undoubtedly accentuate the personality difficulties which in turn will inevitably lead to similar situations. On the other hand, people who find all the problems within themselves, drop below the level of adjustment through self-depreciation. We have then in every situation a series of problems some of which are predominantly relevant to the behaving personality, some to the impeding environment and some to the situation-as-a-whole which includes various forms of relatedness between the individual and his circumstances. Such problems may be classified for purposes of analysis by asking three questions: (a) What part of my personality is here involved about which I need further enlightenment? (b) What further information do I need concerning the various aspects of the impeding environment? (c) What do I need to know about the nature of my relatedness to important phases of the circumstances when the situation is viewed as a whole?

With this much preparation or readiness to meet the situation, we may now proceed to its intelligent consideration, assuming of course, that the situation is regarded as one out of which we mean to derive educative experience. A small number of self-dependent individuals possess sufficient perspicacity and diligence to follow the pathway toward action, that is, arrive at solutions for situations which are satisfying to themselves, without further assistance. It is doubtful, however, whether or not their experiences should be called in the highest sense educational. Most of us find ourselves in significant situations which involve others, situations which are explicitly or implicitly social; we might lift ourselves by our own bootstraps but we might also find that we had lifted ourselves out of, above the situation, not through it. Many "self-made" business men find in later years that worship of their maker is not enough; they become almost sentimental in giving credit to their colleagues and workers— after the time has passed when these collaborators might have shared in the attendant creative experiences. Most of us, if we are intent upon making experience yield its intellectual content, need to *discuss* our situations with those who are concerned with us, with those who are likely to be influenced and with those who have special information which is relevant to our needs.

Discussion is more than talk. We think in verbal forms, and on the whole those who are able to vocalize their ideas, transmit them expressively to others, are more likely to live adequately than those who are inarticulate. But mere talking has no more educational content than bellowing, mooing, barking. Conversation may, indeed, turn back upon itself—as it so frequently does among those who use language as a medium of gossip—and come to be a closed circuit: closed with respect to vocabulary as well as ideas. (A persistent demand has come to express ideas in one-syllable words —to popularize; this is one way of circumscribing language. If an idea cannot be accurately expressed in one-syllable words, it is a falsification of the idea to make the attempt; besides, it degrades those who read or listen by depriving them of incentives for making higher uses of language.) Words become habits—whereupon they lose their teaching function. Think of the countless words spoken aimlessly, pointlessly, futilely about that universal subject of conversation, the weather! Nobody does anything about it, as Mark Twain remarked, and in spite of the fact that we have a rapidly-growing science of weather it is probably true that superstition is more rampant in this sphere of thought than in any other save that of death. The talk of most people about weather has gone round and round the circle of sameness until they are unable to make weather-words jump the groove of habit. Consequently they receive no education from a prodigious amount of talk about a fascinating theme. Pointless talk which follows no rules and consists of simple, quick responses proceeding from one person to another may, of course, become extremely entertaining, and this is putting vocal chords and language to good uses; we should, however, value this sort of talk for what it is, namely, recreation, not education. (We might even pay more attention to the playful possibilities of words when used in serious contexts.)

Discussion is organized talk. When two or more persons exchange experiences for the purpose of throwing light upon a situation, and when the confronting of the situation is itself regarded as an educative opportunity, a tacit recognition to the effect that certain rules are to be followed, is present. If, for example, the group exceeds five of six in number, it usually becomes necessary to agree upon a chairman or leader whose functions will be to keep the discussion going, to maintain its direction, to enlist active participation of all members of the group, to point out discrepancies and relations, to sum up arguments, facts and conclusions, et cetera. When discussion is used as method for adult teaching, the teacher becomes group-chairman; he no longer sets problems and then casts about with various kinds of bait until he gets back his preconceived answer; nor is he the oracle who supplies answers which students carry off in their notebooks; his function is not to profess but to evoke—to draw out, not pour in; he performs in various degrees the office of interlocutor (one who questions and interprets), pro-locutor (one who brings all expressions before the group), coach (one who trains individuals for team-play), and strategist (one who organizes parts into wholes and keeps the total action aligned with the group's purpose). The teacher or chairman does not organize discussion—he keeps it in organized channels.[32] Whatever he brings to the group in the form of opinions, facts and experiences must be open to question and criticism on the same terms as the contributions of other participants.

Debates also follow rules but these are of no value to discussion. The debater selects his conclusion in advance and then proceeds to gather facts and opinions to prove his case. His aim is victory, not enlightenment. He represents "militarism in the intellectual life." [33] In debates we can win only by excluding other points of view whereas in discussions we can achieve only by inclusions. Purposeless conversation may have too little point but debate has too much. The naïve assumption that all questions have two sides distorts debates at the outset; every question has as many sides as there are interests involved and no situation is properly confronted until all relevant interests have been considered. "Where a debate makes much of logic, conference makes more of psychology. It deals not so much with arguments as with reasons. The distinction is important. A man's arguments are the reasons that recite well. They do his heart credit, and display his logical head. His reasons—more truly so-called—are things that lie deeper. They are the meaning to him of his own experience." [34] Rules for discussion will consequently be compatible with the fundamental purpose of conference which is, not to defeat any one, but rather to arrive at a joint conclusion. These rules or guides will moreover be consistent with the aim of adult education which is to make "arriving," not concluding, an educative venture. And, one of the more important rules to bear in mind is this: discussion does not solve situations; it reveals experimental roads to action; real solutions are behavioristic not intellectualistic. After we have recognized a situation, analyzed its involved problems and sought for relevant information and experience, we are prepared to envisage the consequences of various lines of action. Ensuing activities are functions of personalities; each person who sets forth to experiment in the light of the direction provided by preceding discussion will experience unique qualities. Education has been forwarded by the group process; subsequent activity brings this educative process within the scope of deeper realities, the realities of necessitous living. Discussion is neither substitute for scientific method nor refuge for those who, being too timid to live experimentally, hide from the actualities of life. Orderly thinking carries us within sight of new departures in behavior—is analogous to hypothesis in scientific method. Activities ultimately validate or invalidate thought, but it is thinking which liberates action from instinctive, habitual forms. Discussion leads to experimental attitudes and also provides a social medium in which experimentalism can count for something. We do not "think through" problems; we act through. Thinking carries us only so far, then action must follow or we become lost in the wilderness of verbalism.

The situation-approach to learning involves, then, (a) recognition of what constitutes a situation; (b) analysis of the situation into its constituent problems; (c) discussion of these problems in the light of available and needed experiences and information; (d) utilization of available information and experience for purposes of (e) formulating experimental solutions; (f) acting upon experimental propositions with a view of testing, and if necessary, revamping the assumptions which discussion has reavealed.* The subject-approach to education, on the contrary, begins by filling the student's mind with specialized sequences of systematized information which he is expected to recall and use in future situations. But, specialized information, content material, will come into the equation of learning with freshness and vigor if it comes when actually needed. Otherwise our activities will be constantly carrying us on into new adjustments while our memories are surfeited with old information.

It will be readily seen that adult education calls for a new kind of text-book as well as a new type of teacher.

---

* These steps have been arranged in the following order in the pamphlet issued by the Inquiry, 129 East 52d Street, New York City, called *Creative Discussion:*
"(1) What situation have we here?
(2) What sort of problem does it show?
(3) What new information does it involve?
(4) What action will set us on towards a solution?"

Under conventional educational systems both teacher and text attempt to make situations fit subjects whereas the demand is to make subjects serve situations. Teachers of youth assume that their function is to condition students for a preconceived kind of conduct; teachers of adults, on the other hand, will need to be alert in learning how the practical experiences of life can enliven subjects. The purpose of adult education is to give meaning to the categories of experiences, not to classifications of knowledge. Specialists who wish to participate in adult learning will need to do considerable collaborating among themselves before they learn how to relate their subdivided knowledge to current situations. It is perhaps true that no single group in modern life stands in greater need of adult education than experts, specialists: those who continue to know "more and more about less and less."

POSTSCRIPT

"There are two ways of taking the present worldwide agitation. We may take it negatively, as an evidence of disintegration, or positively, as a search for new meanings."

—M. C. OTTO.

POSTSCRIPT

MODERN life derives its momentum from three inter-related sources: *science, specialism* and *industrialism.* The combined impact of these forces distinguishes our time from all previous periods of history. We are modern in the sense that our behavior is predominantly a response to scientific discoveries, experts and machine-production. "The world is now faced with a self-evolving system, which it cannot stop." [35] Where will it take us? There is no knowing.

We can be moderately certain of but one conclusion: adjustments to the propelling forces in the modern world cannot be fruitfully achieved until intellectual, moral and spiritual values emerge which are capable of giving direction and meaning to life. Our ideas and our activities now come from science; our ideals are traditional. The forces which impel are dynamic; the means which control are impotent. We still attempt to bring the modern world into the context of unworkable political theory, superannuated ethics, irrational religion and inept education.

Optimistic interpreters explain this hiatus in modern life in terms of time alone: they contend that science and the technologies are merely ahead of our capacities for adjustment—that we will soon catch up; or, if it happens that we never can catch up, that our knowledge of things will always be in advance of our ability to control, we

· may rest content in acknowledging the inevitable "lag." This view furnishes a convenient name for one aspect of the process but, like so many explanations which stop when a suitable symbol has been found, it illumines the theme but slightly. If life is to become merely adjustment *to* the compulsions of science, specialism and industry, the worth of human personality and experience will cumulatively deteriorate. If life is to have more meaning than is implied in making up time, in overcoming lags, we shall need to learn how to make adjustments *of,* not *to;* we shall need to learn how to relate ourselves to material forces in such manner as to produce qualitative differences in both. If thinking can come abreast of doing only retrospectively, that is, long after the doing has exerted its dominant influence, it will be scarcely worth the trouble to learn how to think. If, on the other hand, intelligence is able to expand our powers, utilize our reserve energies in more complete self-expression and creativeness, reveal to us the only freedom of which we are capable, illumine our enjoyments, integrate our personalities and lead us to dynamic fellowship—if, to sum up, intelligence is the price which man is obliged to pay for continuous growth, no effort directed toward its increase can be wasted.

Growth is the goal of life. Power, knowledge, freedom, enjoyment, creativity—these and all other immediate ends for which we strive are contributory to the one ultimate goal which is to grow, to become. And the meaning of life is always an emergent concomitant of striving. Otherwise, life is illusion, for ends which can be achieved—which are conceived in terms of static qualities—leave the self without further incentives to growth. If there is at once a tragic and heroic side to life, it lies in this: there are no realizable ultimate goals which can be reached without depriving us—in the very act of consummation—of their meaning.

Q.—"Does effort become impossible the moment success is seen to be impossible?"

A.—"No. But it at once becomes irrational."

Reply by Forberg: "Unquestionably that is so, if success be the final aim of effort, the goal the final aim of the runner. But what if the striving were a final aim in itself! What if there were no goal to be attained or, what is the same thing for the runner, only a goal set at an infinite distance? What if the goal were there for the sake of the race, not the race for the sake of the goal?"

—FRIEDERICH CARL FORBERG'S
Apologie seines angeblichen Atheismus.

If then the meaning of life is to be discovered in becoming, education can serve as revealor only insofar as the learning process is continuous—coterminous with the functions of personality. Education is superficially conceived when viewed as a preparation for life. Education *is* life.

REFERENCES

Foreword

1. For further elaboration of Danish civilization, see *Denmark, A Co-operative Commonwealth* by Frederic C. Howe, Harcourt 1921; *Farm Life Abroad* by E. C. Branson, University of North Carolina Press 1924; The Folk High Schools of Denmark and the Development of a Farming Community by Begtrup, Lund and Manniche, Oxford University Press, London; and the articles of Joseph K. Hart published in the *Survey:* Will Denmark Disarm? October 1, 1925; The Plastic Years, April 1, 1926; The Secret of the Independent Farmers of Denmark, June 1, 1926.

Chapter I

2. B. A. Yeaxlee, *Spiritual Values in Adult Education;* 2 volumes, Oxford University Press 1925.

Chapter III

3. Edgar A. Singer, *Modern Thinkers and Present Problems;* Holt 1923; p. 278.

4. Same, p. 279.

5. Nikolai Bukharin, *Historical Materialism;* International Publishers 1925; p. 34.

Chapter IV

6. See M. P. Follett, *New State;* Longmans 1920, and *Creative Experience;* 1924.

7. Horace M. Kallen, *Culture and Democracy in the United States;* Boni & Liveright 1924; p. 209.

8. See No. 6.

9. A. D. Sheffield, *Joining in Public Discussion;* Doran 1922.

Chapter V

10. R. G. Gordon, *Personality;* Harcourt, Brace 1926; p. 42.

11. Lloyd Morgan, *Emergent Evolution;* Holt 1923.

12. John Dewey, *Human Nature and Conduct;* Holt 1922.

13. Edwin B. Holt, *The Freudian Wish;* Holt 1915.

14. See No. 6.

15. See No. 10.

16. See No. 12.

Chapter VI

17. *The New Republic,* June 16, 1926.

Chapter VII

18. Charles H. Cooley, *Social Process;* Scribner's 1918; p. 382. (See Chapters XXXII and XXXV.)

19. A. N. Whitehead, *Science and the Modern World;* Macmillan 1926; p. 279-280.

20. *The Way Out,* Essays on the Meaning and Purpose of Adult Education by Lord Haldane, A. E. Zimmern,

Harold J. Laski, Albert Mansbridge and others; Oxford University Press 1923; p. 100-101.

21. Leo Stein, On Teaching Art and Letters; *The New Republic*, March 3, 1926. (See also his Art of Painting, December 2, 1925; Æsthetic Experience, and Knowing and Feeling, March 17, 1926; Art and the Frame, March 24, 1926; Personality and Identification, March 31, 1926; Art and Society, April 14, 1926.

22. John Dewey, *Experience and Nature;* Open Court 1925; p. 358. (See also Chapter IX on Experience, Nature and Art.)

23. Georg Brandes, *Creative Spirits;* Crowell 1923; p. 220.

24. A. A. Goldenweiser, *Early Civilization;* Knopf 1922; p. 183.

Chapter VIII

25. See Modernizing the College, Adolph E. Meyer; *American Review,* Vol. IV, No. 3.

26, See Walter Lippmann's *Public Opinion;* Harcourt 1922; and *The Phantom Public;* 1925.

27. See No. 18; Chapter V, Particularism Versus the Organic View.

Chapter IX

28. C. Delisle Burns, *The Contact Between Minds;* Macmillan 1923; and *Industry and Civilization;* Allen (London) 1925.

29. For a more detailed exposition of this point of view regarding functional groups as representations of interests, see *Social Discovery* by E. C. Linderman; Republic Publishing Company 1924.

30. See No. 9.

Chapter X

31. John Dewey, *How We Think;* Heath 1910; p. 78.

32. For further details in connection with discussion methods, see *Joining in Public Discussion* by A. D. Sheffield; *Foundations of Method* by W. H. Kilpatrick; Macmillan 1925; *Conferences, Committees, Conventions and How to Run Them* by E. E. Hunt; Harper 1925; *The Why and How of Group Discussion* by H. S. Elliott; Association Press 1923; *Creative Discussion* and other pamphlets (published by The Inquiry, 129 East 52d Street, New York City).

33. H. A. Overstreet, *Influencing Human Behavior;* People's Institute 1925; p. 253. See also his Reason and the Fight Image, *New Republic,* December 20, 1922.

34. *Creative Discussion,* p. 16 (published by The Inquiry, 129 East 52d Street, New York City).

Postscript

35. See No. 19; p. 287.

INDEX

INDEX

A

Activity, 68, 69
Activities, 121
Adjusting process, 85
Adjustment, 44
Adjustments, 85, 86, 93, 94, 101, 127
Æschylus, 30
Æsthetics, 55
Æsthetic values, 69
Americans, 35
American art, 66
Amusements, 79
Applied science, 76
Art, 68, 71
Art-collecting, 55
Art impulses, 71
Artistic experience, 69
Artists, 57
Art spirit, 70
Aspirations, 54
Association, 99
Attitudes, 103

B

Bacon, Francis, 23, 24, 29, 30
Beauty, 55, 56, 68
Behavior, 87
Bosses, 79
Brandes, Georg, 70
British Parliament, 76
Bukharin, N., 24
Burns, C. Delisle, 98

C

Capitalism, 25, 49
Capitalist, 15, 16
Casts, hereditary, 85
Cause and effect, 84
Centrality, illusion of, 83
Chairman, 119
Character, 37
Child, 34

Children, 110
Choice, 34
Citizen, 37, 80, 81, 99
Citizenship, 80, 81
Class, 96
Class-consciousness, 96
Classic tradition, 63
Classicism, 66
Coercion, 102
Collective ideals, 70
Collectivism, 96, 97, 101
Collectivity, 95
College, 49
College presidents, 75
Commissions, 80
Communication, 88, 94
Communities, 36
Community, 35, 98
Community process, 58
Compensation, psychic, 79
Conduct, 13
Conference, 121
Conflict, 46, 93, 101, 103
Conflict, creative, 97
Congress, 77
Conversation, 87, 118
Cooley, Charles H., 83
Cortex, 45
Creative discussion, 122
Creative mood, 57, 58
Creativeness, 55, 58
Creativity, 54, 94
Critics, 69
Cultural ends, 64
Cultural ideas, 65
Culture, 65, 71
Curricula, 75, 78
Customs, 29

D

Dancing, 69
Danish Farmer, 40, 56
Debates, 120
Degrees, Academic, 109

[139]

INDEX

Democracy, 82
Denmark, xxviii, xxix, 5, 64, 105
Departments, Governmental, 80
Dewey, John, 45, 47, 69, 115
Dictator, 81
Difference, 36, 37, 89, 102
Differences, 128
Disappointed One, 49
Discipline, 18
Discussion, 117, 119, 120, 121
Disraeli, 23
Divergence, 36
Drama, 69

E

Economics, 48
Educational Opportunities, 19
Egotist, 49
Eighth Grade, 18
Emotions, 67
Employers, 102
Ends, 33, 59
England, 65
Enjoyable Experience, 64
Enjoyment, 63, 64, 70
Enterprises, Collective, 101
Environment, 17, 48, 116
Environment, social, 104
Essay on Liberty, 43
Ethics, 100, 127
Euripides, 29
Europe, 66
Evolution, 67
Examinations, 114
Experience, 6, 7, 16, 17, 87, 89, 109, 110, 111
Experience, Economic, 112
Experience, Educational, 97, 117
Experience, Emotional, 110
Experiences, Creative, 56
Experiment, 17
Expert Functions, 87
Experts, 80, 81, 83, 84, 85, 88, 89
Experts, Technical, 80
Externalism, 85, 89

F

Fact-finding, 16
Facts, 14, 15, 109
Fact-using, 16
Fantasies, 47, 58
Farmer, 95
Feelings, 68
Fellowship, Dynamic, 128
Folk-Expression, 66
Follett, M.P., 38, 45
Forberg, Friedrich Carl, 129
Formalism, 18
France, Anatole, xxvii, 68
Free Will, 43
Friction, 93
Functions, Collective, 104

G

Games, 40, 68
Generalization, 75
Geniuses, 57
Germany, 64
Goals, 129
Goldenweiser, Alexander, 70
Goodness, 17
Gordon, R.G., 45
Government, 80
Government, Parliamentary, 82
Graduate Study, 78
Great Britain, 105
Great Society, 26
Greek Culture, xxix
Group-Mind, 98
Groups, 99, 101, 104, 119
Growth, 110, 128

H

Habits, 17, 118
Habit-Systems, 35
Happiness, 48
Heredity, 48
Higher Life, 65
High School, 18
Holt, Edwin, 45
Honesty, 102
Human Nature, 8, 23, 24, 44

[140]

INDEX

I

Ideals, 47
Imperialism, 26
Incentives, 35
Independence, 24
Individual, 99
Individualism, 94, 95, 96
Individualists, 95
Individualities, 36, 37
Industrial Organization, 26
Industry, 76, 78, 79
Information, 14
Inquiry, 122
Institutions, 104
Integration, 13, 67, 84
Intellectual class, 18
Intellectualism, 67
Intelligence, Native, 104
Intelligence, Functional, 104
Intelligence, 14, 15, 67, 68
Intelligence tests, 47
Interests, 16, 97, 101
Interstate Commerce Commission, 80
Issues, Technical, 80

J

James, William, 35

K

Knowledge, 14, 23

L

Labor, 27
Laws of Nature, 15
Laymen, 86
Liberalism, 82
Life, Collective, 101
Life-Process, 83
Literature, 66
Logic, 67, 120

M

Machiavellian, 43
Managers, Industrial, 79

Mass Production, 76
Maurice, M. Charles, 68
Meanings, 69, 70, 109
Means, 33, 59
Method, 103
Mill, John Stuart, 43
Mind-Group, 98
Miners, 96
Moralists, 100
Morgan, Lloyd, 45
Municipal Managers, 80
Music, 66
Mussolini, Benito, 82

N

Nationalism, 26
Need, 95
Nietzsche, 49

O

Objectivity, 100
Oculist, 86
One and the Many, 44
Order, Social, 105
Organism, 93
Orientation Studies, 77, 78
Organization, Social, 103
Organism as a whole, 84

P

Pacifists, 99, 100
Painting, 66
Particularists, 83
Pater, Walter, 46
Personality, 34, 38
Pessimism, 23
Phenomena, Social, 98
Philistinism, 63
Politics, 57
Politicians, 102
Play, 39
Ponsonby, Arthur, 45
Power, 23 - 25
Practice, Social, 94
Principles, Ethical, 99
Process, Social, 97, 98, 102

Profit-Production, 49
Prosperity, 35
Psychologists, 13
Psychology, 6, 96
Psycho-Therapy, 46
Public Agencies, 19

R

Reason, 13
Recreation, 39, 79
Relation, 50, 98
Religionists, 102
Renaissance, 75
Response, 16, 98
Revolution, 49
Revolutionists, 48
Revolution of the mind, 26
Rousseau, John Jacques, 43

S

Scholasticism, 75
Schools, 34
Science, 23, 67, 75, 97
Scientific Method, 25
Scientific Subjects, 25
Scientists, 75
Self, 34, 50
Self-expression, 38, 53, 94
Self-improvement, 104
Self-knowledge, 46
Sensibility, 71
Sentimentality, 102
Sentiments, 67
Singer, Edgar A., 23
Situations, 6, 115-116
Situations, Approach, 6, 122
Situation-as-a-whole, 116
Skill, 14
Social Control, 58, 88
Socrates, 30
Society, 43, 44, 101
Social Order, 9
Specialism, 34, 70, 75
Stimulus, 16, 44, 98
State, 76
Specialists, Medical, 84
Structure, Social, 97

Struggle, 93
Struggle-Technique, 27
Subjects, 111, 112
Subject-approach, 113
Subject matter, 6
Subject-teaching, 113
Superstition, 118
Survey Courses, 77
Survival, 101
Synthesis, 36

T

Tariff Commission, 80
Taste, 63
Teachers, 8, 69, 122, 123
Technicians, 79
Technique, Collective, 101
Technologies, 28
Technologists, 80
Textbook, 122
Theory, Social, 94
Thinkers, 85
Thinking, 67, 96, 97
Thinking, orderly, 121
Trade Unionism, 78-79
Trade Union, 27
Thought, 14
Trade Unionists, 57, 99
Traditions, 29
Twain, Mark, 118

U

Unamuno, Miguel, 14
Undergraduate Study, 78
United States, 49, 77, 88
Universities, 76
Utopias, 47, 83

V

Valuations, 110
Values, 16, 100
View, Organic, 84
Vision, 83
Vocational Education, 33
Vocational-Non, 5
Volkshochschulen, xxix
Voting, 38

INDEX

W

Watteau, 46
Western Civilization, 23
Whitehead, A.N., 68
Whitman, Walt, xxx, 7, 40
Wisdom, 30
Words, 118
Workers, 5

Workers' Education, 27
Work's Councils, 79

Y

Yeaxlee, Basil M., 7
Youth, 29, 58
Youths, 54